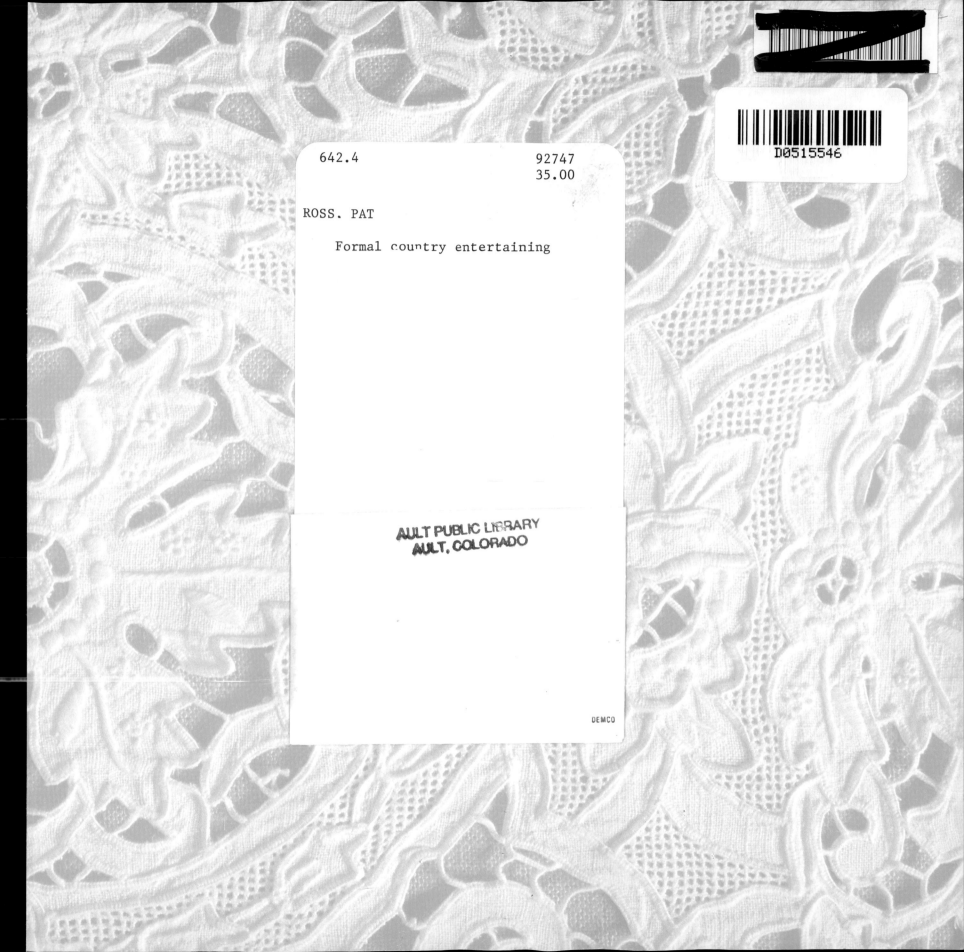

FORMAL COUNTRY ENTERTAINING

AT HOME WITH FAMILY & FRIENDS

Pat Ross

FORMAL COUNTRY
ENTERTAINING

PHOTOGRAPHS BY KEITH SCOTT MORTON

DESIGNED BY RITA MARSHALL

VIKING
STUDIO
BOOKS

Viking Studio Books

Published by the Penguin Group

Viking Penguin, a division of Penguin Books USA Inc.,

375 Hudson Street, New York, New York 10014, U.S.A.

Penguin Books Ltd, 27 Wrights Lane,

London W8 5TZ, England

Penguin Books Australia Ltd, Ringwood,

Victoria, Australia

Penguin Books Canada Ltd, 10 Alcorn Avenue, Suite 300,

Toronto, Ontario, Canada M4V 3B2

Penguin Books (N.Z.) Ltd, 182–190 Wairau Road,

Auckland 10, New Zealand

Penguin Books Ltd, Registered Offices:

Harmondsworth, Middlesex, England

First published in 1992 by Viking Penguin,

a division of Penguin Books USA Inc.

1 3 5 7 9 10 8 6 4 2

Copyright © Pat Ross, 1992

Photographs copyright © Keith Scott Morton, 1992

All rights reserved

Library of Congress Cataloging in Publication Data

Ross, Pat, 1943–

Formal country entertaining : at home with family & friends / Pat

Ross : photographs by Keith Scott Morton : design by Rita Marshall.

p.   cm.   Includes index.

ISBN 0-670-83809-8

1. Entertaining. 2. Cookery, American. I. Title.

TX731.R65   1992

642'.4 — dc20   92-997

Printed in Singapore

Contents

We Wish To Thank

vi

ACKNOWLEDGMENTS

Anticipating Company

2

AN INTRODUCTION

Formal Impressions

7

A TOUCH OF THE DRAMATIC

23

CELESTIAL INSPIRATION

33

SAUSALITO STYLE

Dressed-up Country

47

DECEPTIVELY SIMPLE

59

SHABBILY CHIC

71

DOWN HOME

Al Fresco

85

GARDEN SPOTS

99

COUNTRY INFLUENCES

113

MOVABLE FEASTS

Weekend Company

129

GRACIOUS HOSPITALITY

143

A CHEF IN THE FAMILY

153

DESIGNING WAYS

165

ALL THE BEST INTENTIONS

Regionally Inspired

181

TREE TOPS

191

THEIR OWN SANTA FE

Celebrations

205

A GENEROSITY OF SPIRIT

215

CHRISTMAS AT DAYBREAK

233

A FAMILY FOURTH

From Their Tables

248

THE RECIPES

Resources

268

List of Artisans

279

Recipe Index

280

ACKNOWLEDGMENTS

We Wish

Books are a lot like cakes. You can make one quickly from a mix, and it will look and taste almost like homemade. Or you can start with an empty bowl and make your cake from scratch. When the votes are in, there is nothing quite like homemade.

Formal Country Entertaining is a made-from-scratch book. As the book grew from an idea to a full-fledged undertaking, the network of supportive and enthusiastic people grew in a way that can only be described as a merry geometric progression. Over the course of several years, many staffers, free-lancers, friends, and associates got into the act with heartfelt energy and good wishes.

No one went hungry doing this book, thanks to our creative food people: Susan Quick; Christina Woo at The American Gourmet; Sandra Griswold and Heidi Gintner; Dora Jomassen; Ina Garten at The Barefoot Contessa; Jan Robinson and Lori Banks-Hurley at The Bountiful Board; Elaine Jones and the regulars at Vickie's Veggies; and Stephanie Gans, who joined in on the home stretch.

For coming to our rescue by phone, and on crash schedules, thanks go to: Jane Rivkin and her thoughtful Kitchen Classics staff; our many friends at Terra Cotta, with special

appreciation to Laura Zdeb for her daffodil topiary on page 17; Valerie Cox, formerly of Thaxton & Company; Gary Yee and Morgan Allard at Adrien Linford; the staff of Sue Fisher King; Britt Isham and the staff of The East Hampton Polo Country Store; Dottie Arnold and Libby Esposito at Saratoga Trunk Antiques; Jean Sinenberg at Georgica Creek Antiques; Fisher's Antiques; Lesia Eutsler at Hudson Street Papers; Abby Fleming, Mary Gotavitch, and Thom McDavitt at The Amagansett Plant & Flower Shop; Barbara Rugoff at Fieldcrest Cannon, with special thanks for the Adrienne Vittadini Imperial Damask sheets used on page 144; Barbara Tisdale, for making those sheets into a tablecloth and napkins; Frank McIntosh and Kate Graham at the Frank McIntosh boutique at Henri Bendel; Wendy Nelson at La Serviette for coming through for us so often; Teda and George Balasses, along with Mary Kernell and Amy Ayre, at Balasses House Antiques; Laura Fisher Antiques, for being so consistently thoughtful; Alice McDonald at East Hampton's Bermuda Party Rentals, with special thanks for the tablecloth on page 183; Laurie

Cotter, for the 1950s glasses on page 56; and Maria Brennan at The Grand Acquisitor.

For the occasional cow that needed handling, our thanks to Matthew Freund of Freund's Farm in East Canaan, Connecticut, and his capable cowhands. Doug Cassidy, Susan Cassidy, and Arthur Tiedemann of Southhampton orchestrated our wonderful dog picnic.

The contribution of American artisans played an important role throughout the book. Extra credit goes to: Arabelle Taggart, for whipping up the vintage tablecloth that appears in our jacket photograph; Joyce Ames, for the pretty plate cover on page 131; Two Women Boxing, for the guest book on page 213; and Lindean Mill Glass of Scotland, for the champagne glasses on page 174.

Keith Scott Morton and I were supported by a stellar group of talented associates. On the photography side, thanks are owed to: Ann Gridley Graves (we used her wonderful pumpkin shots on pages 213 and 258), Debra DeBoise (our lively staff shot on the jacket flap is Debra's), Meleda Wegner, Rafael Cuevas, J. R. Rost, Philip Wei, and Jaclene Kirkwood. Walter Wick was kind enough to allow us the use of his birdcage shot on page 47. On the editorial end, we are grateful to: Arlene Kirkwood, for her

To Thank

creative thinking and dedication; Jennifer Holme, for keeping the home fires burning; Julie Robinson, for her calligraphy; Leisa Crane, for the up-to-the-minute resources section; and Patricia O'Shaughnessy, for her elegant styling of selected locations, especially the lovely Christmas and Thanksgiving parties.

My busy and thoughtful agent at Writers House, Amy Berkower, looks out for me with the help of Fran Lebowitz and Michele Rubin. My wonderful publisher at Viking Studio Books, Michael Fragnito, and simpatico editor, Barbara Williams, do the same. Other Viking friends include Martha Schueneman and Sue Scully-Starace; Cathy Hemming; Paul Slovak, Debbie Kwan, and Giulia Melucci in publicity; and Julie Hansen in subsidiary rights.

That leaves family and friends, who somehow always manage to get mentioned last but who always come first in our hearts: Joel and Erica Ross, who are used to sharing me; the patient Christine Churchill, who became Christine Churchill-Morton during Keith's only week off!; Geri Williams, Nancy Hayes, Moira Garvey, Laurel Doody, Roberta Sherman, and Lyn Hutchings; Marie DiManno at the Museum of American Folk Art; Leah Sklar, Angus Wilkie; Jack and John Kirkwood,

who contributed their brawn; Carolyn Gore-Ashe, Holly Horton, Gail Rock, and Gene Heil; Hermenia Young, who is always backstage; and Franny and Dick Zorn, the quintessential hosts.

Keith and I consider Rita Marshall a kindred spirit for bringing our words and our images together so elegantly and respectfully with her design, and, for this, we extend to her our sincere gratitude.

Several years ago I attended a party at which the entertainment was a psychic who looked into the guests' futures. Sadly, I have not come into the unexpected sum of money she promised, unless I count the odd singles I recently discovered in the pocket of an old coat. Fortunately, however, I believe that one of her predictions did come true: "You will work with a man who has hair the same color as yours." Is it simply coincidence that both Keith Scott Morton and I have manes generously flecked with silver? Or was it in the stars? Whatever the explanation, I am fortunate to have worked with this extraordinarily gifted and good-natured person on not one but two books now, sharing the ideas, the bur-

dens, and, I hope, the praise for our shared vision.

Our lives were constantly enriched by people who would somehow appear, as if by magic, offering countless gestures of friendship—a place to stay, a meal to share. One such person was Thomas Von Covenhoven, who cheerfully arrived at the Parsons home in Los Angeles with an armful of flowers and a willing heart. Without fanfare, Thomas busily arranged and potted, and made his natural talent look easy. Sadly, our friend Thomas's life ended last year. All of us who knew him—briefly or for a lifetime—are sorry that Thomas did not live long enough to see the beauty of his work in these pages, but his creations remain here for our fond remembrance.

IN MEMORIAM
THOMAS VON COVENHOVEN
1948-1991

Anticipating

Company

AN INTRODUCTION

When my book *Formal Country* was published in 1989, the term I had coined for an emerging decorating style appeared to be a contradiction in terms. Yet when understood as the elegance of traditional formality combined with the warmth and charm of country style, "formal country" suddenly made perfect sense. It seems that both men and women who seek an eclectic decorating style for their busy lives were happy to find a book that said it was okay to break a few old rules. Four years later, "formal country" no longer requires a definition. And,

happily, the term has come to describe more than a decorating style. It has also come to characterize a life-style embraced by many of us when we entertain.

It seems that childhood memories have made an indelible impression on the entertaining styles of many of the home owners in this book. Most of the people I talked with spoke of early influences: a mother whose home-made cakes were legend, a father whose tomato crop kept the family in tomato soup through the cold winter months, people who were never inconvenienced by setting an extra place at their tables. In going back to their roots, people today often copy their mothers, grandmothers, or, less frequently, the men in their family who felt comfortable in the domestic quarters of the home. No idea is really new: it's based on some memory, some idea that has gone before and been freshened up or embellished. And bringing entertaining into the nineties is the idea that even formal entertaining can be enlivened with country-style warmth.

Writing *Formal Country* and *Formal Country Entertaining* gave me a valid excuse to peek into the cupboards and pantries of other people's homes. The eighteen profiles in these pages show eighteen unique personal styles, each one spontaneous and filled with a welcome exchange of ideas. The common denominator is a belief that home entertaining should and can be a pleasure for both guests and hosts.

There are no extravaganzas, no Herculean culinary feats, no need to win the lottery to set a pretty table, no need to perform for royalty. Happily, the home owners in this book offer no universal blueprint for entertaining, yet the occasions they celebrate here inspire the rest of us to give it a try. The lighthearted touches, romantic fancies, and old-fashioned good times offer up a variety that is truly the spice of life.

Keith Scott Morton and I paid special visual attention to the many wonderful details of entertaining that we found: cheerful, top-heavy flowers popped into miniature medicine bottles; a sparkling lineup of mismatched wine glasses; the way a collection of pottery mixes and matches on a handsome pine table; a romantic glow of candlelight from an iron chandelier; bright nasturtiums transforming an ordinary salad into an artful arrangement; a primitive barn-wood table adorned with elegant textiles and the finest bone china in a worldly play of opposites. Such lovely images excite our senses and spark our own ideas.

The most memorable occasions are often the most spontaneous ones, born of necessity or sheer whimsy. A friend tells of an evening in July when a group of friends organized a last-minute picnic for a concert on the village green. He was put in charge of plates and other paper necessities but, alas, his supply cupboard was bare. Then he remembered the party things in the attic—brightly colored plates adorned with Santa faces, red napkins to match, snowball candles, a few broken candy canes, and a package of holiday streamers. On the hottest night of the summer, the thoughts of December kept the temperature right. The person in charge of dessert was equally inspired: Popsicles were kept frosty in a cooler.

My childhood introduction to group entertaining was the covered-dish suppers at our local church. I don't recall that there was any real coordination, yet somehow all the courses seemed to show up, and in the right quantities. Mother's specialty was pot roast—her English-Irish version of my father's favorite German sauerbraten. The term "groaning board" might well have originated with such a supper, for several long tables from the Sunday school rooms were placed end to end. As the dishes arrived, they were set down in no particular order, with little space in between—a feast of bubbling casse-roles, preserved farm products, fresh vegetables, and desserts enough to break a fat man's heart. I recall the satisfied faces, the community spirit, and the way my mother beamed when the compliments came her way. Looking back, I wonder if the meat might have been a little dry and the potatoes a little soggy. But none of that mattered, for it was the atmosphere that counted, and the feeling of being together.

The deadlines for this book have been met, but I still have difficulty realizing that my work is complete. At a party I attended just last week, sunflowers arranged in galvanized tin pails were so picture perfect that I wanted to include them in the book. A small supper for friends where the host ordered Indian take-out food and we sat cross-legged on the floor and ate from shallow wooden bowls will have to go uncelebrated. Wedding buffet napkins made by pinking the edges of soft muslin squares will never appear in these pages! Suddenly I am surrounded by original table settings, lovely flower arrangements, and delectable recipes that must go unsung! But, then, I think, isn't this what Formal Country Entertaining is all about, everyday creativity, and find-ing extraordinary new ideas in ordinary situations?

I know I've taken my own advice when I search the September garden for something to arrange. Only last week, a hurricane devastated our entire garden, leaving us with only a few hearty flowers, a bumper crop of basil gone to flower, and ivy that will outlive us. Our admiring dinner guests wondered where we found such a thoroughly unusual arrangement: giant marigolds gracefully bent from the wind, flowering herbs, and trailing ivy looking natural together in a tall white pitcher. Then I

remembered a favorite line from *The Wizard of Oz:* "You've always had the power. . . ."

Formal

Impressions

A Touch of the Dramatic

D eborah Parsons brought a share of Montana hospitality with her when she moved to Los Angeles, a city known for its glitz. "Billings is the most sophisticated city in Montana," she cheerfully informs visitors, who expect to find cowboy boots and tumbleweed among her belongings. At first, the elegant canyon home with a Hollywood mogul's view of the city would seem as far from Montana as the moon. Deborah and her husband, Craig, who works in corporate public relations, bought the modest sixties house for its spectacular site and for the landscaping—tropical fruit trees and a lush garden that winds from the terraces surrounding the house down the hillside for nearly a mile. Their renovation included opening up the downstairs living area into one large room (with frequent entertaining in mind), whitewashing the dark wood walls, and finishing all the floors in light pickled pine. With this airy backdrop, the drama of L.A. came together with the warmth of the country.

Deborah and Craig Parsonses' home offers an idyllic West Coast welcome. Both the weather and the house are perfectly suited to indoor-outdoor entertaining. Heavy floor-to-ceiling windows may be opened onto the entrance deck, providing a glimpse of the dining room within.

At sunset, luminarias placed on each step of the entrance shed needed light. These large votive candles are perfect for creating festive and romantic moods. They burn slowly and can be used again and again.

Entertaining is clearly Deborah's domain, and she comes by it naturally. Her mother baked a cake a day for Deborah and her three sisters and the trail of friends who followed them home after school. Traditional family gatherings and holiday times were considered sacred to the extent that every occasion had its own set of dishes. Deborah recalls green Christmas plates, Easter plates with a rabbit design, and Thanksgiving plates with a cornucopia in the center. "I bought my first set of china when I was in the eighth grade," she recalls. "It was a pattern called Arcadia and I bought it on the installment plan, earning money vacuuming a local shop after school. I've outgrown the look, but I can't part with the china."

It bothers this family that holidays are passed over so lightly in California, where seasonal changes go unnoticed. They remedy that by making a great fuss over occasions both at home and at Terra Cotta, Deborah's decorative-accessories shop, which is filled with the same wonderful garden furniture, antiques, floral arrangements, and collectibles that fill her home and grace her table.

A miniature house has become a part of the garden.

Deborah has earned her nickname: "The Queen of Excess." Concerned that customers or guests might lack for something, she provides a predictable overabundance that is the butt of good-natured joking among family and friends. "I just can't do anything on a small scale, so we generally invite a crowd," says Deborah, whose charm and candor are appreciated by her guests.

It's the thoughtful details of these parties that make the difference. Celebrations large and small all rate a thoughtful invitation—a pretty handwritten card, a note on heavy paper that in itself feels impressive, or plain card stock embellished with decorative seals, which Deborah buys by the roll. Friends who do calligraphy are happy to write out individual invitations—or, when the guest list is a long one, a master that can be duplicated. There's a flower arrangement on every table; *luminarias* light the pathway from the canyon road; bowls of pot-

H eavy
Victorian doors belie the
modern interior of the
house, a creative renova-
tion that infused a sixties
design with traditional elegance. Terraces only a
brief walk from the front
door are planted with lush
tropical plants and flowers.

pourri, fruit, and nuts stand in the entrance hall; antique linen hand towels, starched and pressed, wait in the powder room. Friends are accustomed to finding a pianist seated at a small upright off the living room, where he plays old favorites all evening long.

Party-giving is rarely solitary for Deborah, who wastes no time getting everyone into the spirit of things, especially her sister and business associate, Pat, and their witty friend Thomas, a floral designer who frequently makes a house gift of his talent. Son Taylor is occasionally pressed into service as a waiter or a roving photographer. With the same efficiency and decisiveness that make her a good businesswoman, Deborah directs and organizes events from casual brunches to catered dinners. Her energy is boundless and her spirited Montana hospitality has traveled well.

Deborah has set out an anytime-you're-up breakfast buffet on the terrace with warm Lazy Banana Blueberry Muffins (recipe, p. 248) and fresh-squeezed orange juice in festive sherry glasses. A flat basket tray is used for carrying as well as for serving.

The fabric remnants covering the table make no pretense of being a tablecloth, with a selvage edge still showing. Deborah likes the way fabric by the yard drapes gracefully, then launders and stores easily, without limiting itself to only one table size.

The renovation of the house took into careful account the Parsonses' desire for thoughtfully planned conversational seating throughout the main floor of the house. "We look like a sofa ad," jests Deborah, "but it's terrible to make guests stand for hours and juggle buffet plates." Their much-envied view is barely hidden by soft gauzelike curtains that add a formal touch without detracting from the panorama.

A low pine map chest doubles as a coffee table, a generous surface for a casual brunch. Simplicity is the key: an easy and delicious Egg-and-Sausage Soufflé and Papaya Salad with Tangy Dressing (recipes, p. 248) are served directly from an oversized basket lined with a fresh vintage pillow sham. Deborah owns dozens of soft cotton checked napkins; they seem to go with everything and need no ironing.

R*ed wine vinegar with herbs in bold glass cruets makes an effective table decoration. A place mat with a coordinating napkin is arranged on top of an antique woven cloth set with white embossed Italian dinnerware. A gift card becomes a place card when tucked in a tiny moss-filled pot.*

Deborah is fond of the
lovely Limoges dinnerware
designed by her friend Bill
Goldsmith. An appealing
fruit pattern echoed by the
dessert berries stands out
against an antique paisley
shawl used in place
of a tablecloth.

A mag-
nificent cymbidium orchid
fills a pot painted black
and edged in gold leaf. The
oval table is French, just
high enough to hold food
and drink during the cocktail hour. The laurel-leaf
wall sconces provide soft
light in the hallway.

*A treasured old album
filled with photographs of
an anonymous family—a
souvenir from a Parisian
flea market—lies open on
an old pine trunk in the
hall, beckoning guests to
leaf through the pages.
Pungent potpourri fills an
original Shaker sifter and
mixes with the sweet smell
of lilacs and tulips. Antiquarian books support an
antique garden urn.*

Deborah's shop on fashionable Montana Avenue is called Terra Cotta, so it follows that her home is filled with assorted pots and vessels containing unusual flower arrangements, both fresh and dried. A small earthenware pot has first been "aged" with green paint, filled with Oasis that has been thoroughly soaked in water, then "planted" with the daffodils. Finally, the stems are tied with French wired ribbon and the Oasis is covered with moss.

Clove-studded pears form a still life on a paisley-covered side table. Candles are lighted long before sunset, which comes late in the evening. A sculptured moss topiary fills a hand-painted pot.

P ractical yet pretty, lead crystal is not nearly as fragile as fine blown glass, so it works well for large buffet dinners, when people must travel with their drinks. The gold-rimmed glasses are Fostoria goblets traced to one of the old copper-king mansions in Montana, and were a gift from Deborah's mother. The other glasses are commonly available Yugoslav lead crystal.

Guests are treated to a delicious and down-to-earth
meal of American Crab
Cakes with Deborah's
Sauce, a Winter Vegetable
Casserole (recipes, p. 249),
and a tossed green salad.
Deborah calls the green
china her "celebration
plates," used for special occasions. A fork and a
spoon are the only utensils
needed for this meal, and
they're handily wrapped in
brocade napkins settled in
a basket. Flowers, water-
cress, and moss dress up
the buffet.

A lthough the mood is elegant, the presentation of the food is relaxed. "I don't want guests to feel intimidated at our table," says Deborah. The cotton-lined bronze silk draperies are pulled to the sides to let in the cool evening breezes.

The crab cakes have been prettily garnished with flowers (for show only) borrowed from nearby arrangements.

The Parsonses' good friend Thomas Von Covenhoven made a gift of his talent as a floral designer by creating a mossy garden of white flowers on the table. Thomas began by placing a row of water-soaked Oasis down the center of the table on heavy black plastic bags. The Oasis is then covered with dampened moss before the flowering bulbs and cut flowers are settled in place.

A warm apple crisp, still in its stainless steel baking dish, is nestled in a shallow basket, and decorated with lemon branches from a tree just outside the door. The dessert will be spooned into large individual ramekins that sit comfortably on laps. The big majolica-style coffee mugs on the buffet have been chosen over delicate cups and saucers, which are difficult to balance. The elegant evening ends on a homey note.

CELESTIAL INSPIRATION

The gracious foyer of Ann and Thayer Bigelow's city apartment is one of three rooms used to seat people when the couple entertains a crowd. Guests lucky enough to dine here enjoy an original wall design by the painter Michael Murphy. "Stars, sunbursts, and the moon in all its phases are whimsical and lighthearted," says Ann.

A shop may be crammed with run-of-the-mill collectibles, but if there is one unusual object hidden in a corner and overlooked, Ann Bigelow will find it —and at a good price. A former fashion forecaster who now runs a successful corporate gift-buying service, this hostess spots what's on the cutting edge by sheer instinct. "I like new things, quick change, whimsy," Ann readily admits, with the same dry wit that she brings to her refreshingly original yet rather traditional style of entertaining.

Guests entering the foyer of the sprawling city apartment belonging to Ann and her husband, Thayer, im-

Sometimes the best gifts are the ones never given! Ann couldn't part with these painted-tin monkey candelabra, so she had to substitute another gift for newlywed friends. Here, the monkeys shed light on a delicately faded topiary.

mediately sense that urban elegance is tempered with Ann's flair for trend setting. The walls of the foyer—a room used for entertaining guests as well as greeting them—have been stippled a warm Chinese red, then gilded with whimsical moon and star images, the first hint of a subtle celestial theme that is repeated throughout the apartment. Ann and Thayer, the president of a cable network, prefer entertaining at home—even for corporate occasions—because it "puts people at ease and extends a kind of personal access that meeting in some restaurant can never accomplish." There's an eclectic and revealing mix of possessions on every available surface: dozens of

Celestial
Salad
· with pommery vinaigrette ·
Roasted Pork
Rosemary
and baby squash
Nutty Wild Rice
Fruit Sorbet
Lemon Bundt
Cake with Apricots.

family photos, stacks of art and travel books, a comprehensive tape and CD collection, and countless decorative objects that Ann feels are "expressive of us." Because the objects are so tastefully selected, guests undoubtedly ask about them—especially the Aztec sun wall sculpture (found on a trip to Mexico), and the antler chandelier (from the time when the family considered moving to Denver).

No matter the size of the party, Ann procrastinates until the day of the event. "I tend to work only under pressure, so from ten A.M., I'm whirling!" An instinctively good cook, Ann finds it difficult to share recipes: her "dash of this" and "a cup or so" of that defy quantification. Ann's least favorite meal is the traditional roast meat, vegetables, and potatoes; however, it's the one she always serves because, as she says, "I'm more familiar and secure with this type of cooking." Once she tackled a six-course Indian dinner—very hot and delicious—for good friends with some success. "Only one dinner guest asked for peanut butter and jelly!"

Ann's advice for enjoying larger affairs: hire someone to serve and help with the dishes if you can. As for Thayer's role: "He opens the wine!" Thayer, who could easily win a contest for the most congenial host of the year, agrees that his role does not really begin until the first guest arrives.

The final hour finds Ann checking the seasonings and searching for votive candles. Ann owns an ample supply of small glass vases, so if she's short on time and planning, she simply fills them with roses and places them "all around." One guest tells of putting her coat on an unmade bed, "but the sheets were so pretty and the party was such fun, who cared?" Which is the point of being entertained by the Bigelows, in whose home one of the suns is always winking.

A charming painted lead frame is put to good use displaying the evening's menu.

Ann couldn't resist copying this humorous Victorian etching onto fine bond stationery for dinner invitations. "I knew the friends we were inviting would remember the dinner we gave where, without warning, a fragile chair collapsed and a guest landed on the floor, unhurt but startled," she said.

Tall storage cupboards in this solidly built prewar building hold sufficient china and silverware—passed along from both sides of the family—for large gatherings. Two silverware patterns are mixed. Subtly adorned Limoges plates are reproductions of Chinese export patterns, and are set off by handsome gilded chargers. Extra lengths of the gold thread used in the floral arrangement are wound around crisp Battenberg lace napkins. A Celestial Salad with Pommery Vinaigrette (recipe, p. 250) seems fitting.

Another Victorian etching, found in a book, becomes a place card. A dried "hedge" of wheat, lavender, and roses forms the centerpiece. The substantial wineglasses are by the Vermont glassmaker Simon Pearce.

FRANKLIN

Ann says she rarely uses a cloth on her heavy cherry table, a contemporary reproduction of an Italian antique. She prefers the beauty of the wood and feels that guests are sometimes hampered by "too many linens in the way." The Regency-style armchairs are a handsome match for the table. A comfortable sofa expands the dining room's possibilities.

T*he floral designer Roberta Bendavid created this dried flower arrangement when Ann discovered that water would cause her treasured mercury glass bowl to "melt." A set of blue–rimmed plates from Tiffany's, a wedding gift to Ann's mother many years ago, is used in combination with new china that features tiny stars on its wide burgundy rim. Ceramic fruit by Barbara Eigen are perfect containers for a sherbet course, which can be made and frozen ahead of time.*

An early elmwood drop-leaf table in the living room serves as a sofa table during the day, a dining table with a city view at twilight. Some lucky guest will get the comfortable wing chair. Before the entree is passed, everyone has a moment to enjoy the hand-painted Italian plates, each with a different musical-instrument motif. Two colored raffia place mats with gold borders are used together under each oversized plate.

Once again, dried flowers —also called "everlastings" for the enduring pleasure they give—grace the table. Although the Bigelows like the effect of candlelight, they shy away from rooms that are "too dark and too like a night club." Here, tin-leafed votives from a garden shop and a pair of elaborate candle lamps highlight the arrangement.

*C*elestial-
motif dessert plates by the
ceramic designer Ann
Marie Murray seem pre-
destined for this household!
The antique demitasse set
and silver service are fam-
ily treasures. A plain
bundt cake has been
dressed up with Lemon
Glaze (recipe, p. 251) and
Turkish apricots. Sprigs of
heather and greens have
been added for decoration.

Ann prefers a still life of
beautiful pears in a simple
wire basket on the coffee
table instead of an affected
arrangement that "would
look more at home in the
Roman Empire."

Nestled in the hills above Sausalito a short distance from the Golden Gate Bridge, Sue Fisher King's recently renovated bungalow has barely had time for the paint to dry. "A couple of weeks ago, I was ready to just plow it under and start over!" exclaims

Sue Fisher King was immediately drawn to a large glass-fronted storage cupboard that she saw in a British magazine. It seemed grand enough to store most of her tasteful tabletop accessories — both old and new — and open enough to show them off. Sue clipped the page and then, years later, used the picture as a model for her own cupboard, which she had built into the far end of the kitchen, facing the dining area.

Sue to newly arrived guests, who are still pondering the reliability of their parking brakes on these treacherous hills. The conversation quickly turns to Sue's former "plain Jane cottage," which has been transformed into her dream house—or the promise of one. With her usual dramatic flair, Sue recounts the myriad tasks that still need her attention.

The cupboard is filled with what Sue wryly refers to as "my mixed-up junk." There's a special collection of hand-painted plates, a ceramic lion candle holder used alone or with its mate, and delicately painted Danish cookware holding lemons from the yard. The owner's irreverence about her possessions does not hide the great pride she feels about the many tasteful and unique tabletop accessories she's devoted years to acquiring.

("I have to find fabric for that second bedroom, and get the plumber back, and . . .") Nonetheless, a few unfinished details do not prevent this spirited and energetic hostess from inviting friends over to celebrate.

The main part of the house seems custom made for an easy flow of guests. The living, dining, and kitchen areas open graciously into each other, sharing a sweeping view of Richardson Bay. The owner of the San Francisco home-accessories shop and wholesale business that bears her name, Sue Fisher King is a consummate entertainer. "I shop," says Sue. "That's what I love to do!" And she shops for the many special touches that make her entertaining tasteful and memorable.

C ut hothouse arrangements are unnecessary when lush garden plants and bright flowers are in perpetual bloom just a few steps outside the door. Faithfully tended by Sue and a friend who is also a devoted gardener, the garden begins on the deck, in planters and decorative urns, then cascades heedlessly down the hillside property. Here, a large terra-cotta garden urn from Italy has been pulled indoors for added color and atmosphere.

To take full advantage of the view of Richardson Bay, Sue placed her antique Biedermeier table and chairs in the dining area, by the windows. The fine patina of the bare wood combined with the striking design of the dinner plates make tablecloths and place mats unnecessary.

Harmonious blending is what Sue advocates—mixing heirlooms, new acquisitions, textures, colors, periods, styles. A tall cupboard, a prominent feature of the kitchen, contains family heirlooms—souvenir spoons collected by three generations, antique china from England and France, an imaginative assortment of candle holders—plus all the new "stuff" that Sue finds during her travels in France and Italy. She appreciates the meaningful eccentricities of handcrafted accessories. The history surrounding her stunning collection of dinnerware from Siena makes for lively dinner conversation, which is probably just what Sue intended.

Sue prefers seated gatherings, "so you can put your elbows on the table and really gab." The table—Biedermeier with a lovely veneer—has been placed in front of the windows for the view and the breeze. She's happy

Sue doesn't wait for a soup course to show off her elegant soup tureen from France. Ask Sue for her definition of an ideal evening and, without hesitation, she'll tell you it's an early supper at home for six to eight good friends who can enjoy the sunset and the cool bay breezes.

when her guests linger over a meal that she has spent "all day" preparing. "I consider anything not made by me cheating!" she says, scoffing at the notion that she might pick up dinner on the way home, even if her guest list numbers forty-eight, the most she's comfortable cooking for. "After that," she adds, "an occasion turns into an extravaganza!"

Sue never sends out invitations; she'd rather phone and be secure in knowing the invitation arrived. Hearty peasant food is her first choice—French or Italian. A good stew or a gumbo fills the bill, frequently served right from the stove, a brand-new six-burner Viking range that is her definition of "designer label." Her music of choice is show tunes, robust selections that always trigger memories and singing along.

Whether the occasion is a fabulous dinner for many, or tea and scones for a few, Sue advises customers and friends alike to "invite people you like, provide comfortable seating so they don't go home early, spend time on the food so they don't go home hungry, then join your own party and forget who's giving it!" Happily, Sue is a hostess who takes her own good advice.

Jasmine and ivy trail from inexpensive plaster urns that are simple to sponge-paint and give the table arrangement height and grace. A home-furnishings retailer and importer, Sue uses many of the tabletop accessories she designs and sells, including these sturdy glasses from Italy, in her home. Her white cotton damask napkins add texture yet allow the colorful plates to take center stage. Napkin rings relate to shapes in the plates and to the metal of the flatware.

These stunning plates are usually the center of attention, treating guests to a bit of Italian feudal history. Each plate is hand-painted with a different design — or emblema — representing each of seventeen separate districts of the city-state of Siena. Intense competition, including wildly dangerous horse races in which bareback riders wear their district colors proudly, still exists among districts today.

Sue believes that everyone is allowed a little extravagance now and then. In this case it's the handmade stainless and faux-ivory flatware, a much-admired French import.

A hearty supper of Chicken and Shrimp Gumbo (recipe, p. 250) will be served buffet style right from its earthenware pot on the stove. The colorful mix of vegetables used in the gumbo has taken on a second role, as a decorative arrangement. One by one, guests ladle the steaming gumbo into shallow bowls, then top it with rice, sundae style. In the kitchen, the line between hostess and guest disappears.

T
he Viking stove, one that any professional chef would envy, was a must for Sue when she renovated her kitchen "to keep myself happy." Accompaniments to the gumbo — rice with peas and Buttermilk Corn Sticks (recipe, p. 251) — stand at the ready on a nearby burner. A dessert of Peach Walnut Crisp (recipe, p. 251) stays warm on the stainless-steel shelf.

The world's easiest and most delicious coleslaw, named "Confetti" for its festive appearance, is set out on a kitchen counter (recipe, p. 251).

*Q*ueenie, Sue's spunky Jack Russell terrier, moves like the wind and wastes no time check-ing out unattended bags. Guests are generally amused by the coat rack, a tribute to Queenie's impor-tance in this household!

A low chest of drawers in the living room becomes a dessert buffet. Guests are offered a choice of desserts — the warm peach crisp, individual fruit tarts, or both. Handsome star-shaped plates are paired with a demitasse set that shares the stellar motif.

Travel memories from two generations are lovingly documented in these souvenir and commemorative spoons, collected by Sue's grandparents and parents and now cherished by her. Guests have their choice of simple, engraved silver spoons from the 1893 World's Fair or from cities like Denver and Omaha, or more elaborate spoons of silver with cloisonné and delft. Whether the guest list numbers two or twenty, Sue sets out the entire collection on an engraved silver tray.

Dressed-up

Country

DECEPTIVELY SIMPLE

A mud room, which here bears no resemblance to its inelegant name, is a cheerful entranceway for guests at Linda Cheverton's and Walter Wick's cottage-style home. An impromptu arrangement of pine cones and evergreens, combined with dried hydrangeas, celebrates the season. The large painted tin Tree of Life candelabrum is Mexican in origin, from the 1930s. During the holidays, Linda and Walter light the tiny candles.

There's an easy southern style in this New England home, where generous servings of down-home food miraculously appear when a few extra guests arrive. Friends often show up unexpectedly, much to the homeowners' delight, perhaps to drop off a bunch of flowers, deliver a basket of fresh peaches, or share a tip about the country antiques show. Linda Cheverton's Mississippi traditions have traveled north with her: blessed with genuine grace and a soft-spoken manner, Linda and Walter Wick, her equally congenial photographer husband, rarely stand on ceremony when greeted with the opportunity to welcome friends into their home, by invitation or by chance.

The bird cages only hint at the extent of Linda Cheverton's passion for collecting.

Linda Cheverton is at a distinct advantage when it comes to setting a pretty table. As a prop stylist for gourmet-food magazines, her business is all about table-top arrangements. As a result, her cupboards and drawers are filled with recent discoveries and long-held treasures—the many props she uses in her business that are "on loan" to her private life. "I see entertaining as a way to show off some favorite table settings, experiment a bit, and let others enjoy them as much as we do," says Linda, who frequently treats a dinner for two as a company occasion.

Always willing to share a few trade secrets, Linda expresses a special fondness for early-twentieth-century art pottery that "just seems to work well with everything," especially 1930s English pottery, which she and Walter like to "mix up with contemporary pieces." But it's difficult to pin down the eclectic mix that Linda and Walter have collected, including antique wire baskets ("great for bread"), fine silver flatware ("loved and used every day for every occasion"), and the extraordinary collection of antique bird cages that command center stage. When Linda simply ran out of drawers and cupboards for her many acquisitions, she began to exhibit at antiques shows, where others may now delight in her good taste.

The only home scents that fill the Cheverton-Wick home are natural ones—fresh flowers and savory foods. Linda spends so much time every day around gourmet food, styling it and sampling the shots, that she and Walter welcome simple meals flavored with fresh herbs. Lunch for close friends might mean a pleasing Cobb salad—crisp Bibb lettuce, crumbled blue cheese, bits of smoked ham, all sprinkled with dill—or tasty melted-cheese sandwiches and grilled vegetables with the unexpected addition of sage. An herb bouquet of basil, chive blossoms, or oregano flowering beyond its peak is often pretty and fragrant on their table in a small creamer, a jelly glass, or even a teacup.

Linda decorates every room with flowers, presented in fresh and spontaneous arrangements in unusual con-

A frequently invited friend brought a gift of parrot tulips, anemones, viburnum, and baby hydrangeas, which became a graceful springlike bouquet in Linda's 1930s American Brush Pottery vase. Potted miniature daffodils are a further reminder of an approaching spring.

T he 1952 painting by the American artist Charles Preston echoes other patterns, colors, and themes in the breakfast room, a popular place to linger over coffee or enjoy a hot lunch on a winter day.

tainers. She rarely stops with the flowers, though, frequently adding surprising natural elements—smooth pebbles, sea glass, spongy moss, shells, and berries. Autumn leaves, collected during a walk in the woods with Jackson, their Catahoula dog, are sometimes found months later, tucked deeply in the pocket of a favorite jacket.

Whether it's a few friends or a free-for-all, the operative word is "relax." Linda and Walter manage to watch the pots, uncork the wine, and enjoy their company without fuss, muss, or needless expense. They greet company with the assumption that things will be wonderfully simple and their efforts will be appreciated. Happily, this attitude becomes a self-fulfilling prophecy.

Dressed up and shown off, the basic toasted-cheese sandwich is elevated to new heights! Grilled zucchini slices, red peppers, and a sprig of sage add interest to an old favorite (recipe, p. 252).

I t's difficult to find pristine vintage luncheon cloths and a set of coordinating napkins, but this hostess has been busy collecting vintage linens for many years. The contemporary glassware, a warm touch that picks up the blue of the cloth, is hand-blown by Gilmore Glassblowers in New York State.

A hearty Burgundy, fruit, and a variety of cheeses are set out for two near an American birdhouse from the twenties. This couple believes that special entertaining touches ought not be restricted to guests. A time-worn bench is pulled closer to the hearth.

The wine is given a few moments to breathe in antique etched-glass stemware. Linda and Walter feel that cherished pieces of crystal or china need not come in neat sets or be perfectly matched. They are pleased when they come upon even a single piece that appeals to them. Cheverton and Wick are believers in good mixes—of guests and of collectibles!

Leaves in relief are the sole embellishment of this pleasing English Ridgway china. One of nature's found objects — a log covered with lichen and woodland mosses — has become a table decoration. An ivy topiary is trimmed with baby crab apples, dried hydrangeas, dried moss, and an occasional gum ball.

Linda has filled a glass pedestal with sugared fruit — a sort of Sugarplum Fairy centerpiece — using two Simon Pearce glass cake plates for the first and second tiers and an antique glass compote for the top tier. Sugaring fruit is simple: beat egg whites until frothy, dip in clean fruit, then quickly roll the fruit in fine granulated sugar. A hard crust forms as the egg white dries, looking almost too perfect to disturb.

Linda's favorite china is 1930s English china designed by Susie Cooper. Linda likes Cooper's simple, color-banded work, which goes well with food. Linda and Walter began collecting Cooper china with a few inexpensive, odd pieces found at country antiques shows. Now their place settings number sixteen!

The hand-painted cloth and napkins were done by the artisan Liz Wain especially to complement the Susie Cooper china.

A modest space in the dining room serves as a liquor cabinet and bar, with sets of antique glassware and china lending visual appeal when the cabinet is open.

Juice and jelly glasses from times past—with their colorful animal-character images—are still favorites today.

L ittle is known about the origin of these old household stools, which appear to be awaiting a famous family of bears.

SHABBILY CHIC

The weathered wood furniture in Melinda Reed's sunny kitchen says that no one stands on ceremony here. Early American chairs from Pennsylvania, one a Grange chair, were used in town meetings and must have many tales to tell. The whitewashed plate rack was constructed from barn board and pegs. It's the perfect storage space for books, for the morning paper, and crockery — all within easy reach.

When Melinda Reed was a child, her favorite toys were the tools and supplies from her father's workshop—levels and hammers and wood chips. Her father taught Melinda to plane and to file, to create from scratch. Today, as a designer and maker of country furniture, she can look back with appreciation to days spent with her dad in his shop. Her mother, very much the lady, bemoaned her daughter's rough-and-tumble ways. Melinda remembers her mother lamenting many times over, "Is it necessary to get grass stains on each and every one of your dresses?" According to Melinda, "They finally came to their senses and accepted the fact that I could not be neat and correct. Well, I *could* be, but most often I chose not to be!"

Chloe and Ruddy stake out a favorite easy chair in the kitchen, which Melinda has draped with yards of cotton fabric brought home from the Greek island of Patmos.

Now, as an adult and owner of Fox Hill Furniture, Melinda entertains with a style that harks back to her childhood philosophy: don't take things too seriously, have a sense of humor, and, most important, make sure everyone relaxes and has a good time. Spontaneity is Melinda's natural style when she opens her modest Connecticut farmhouse to friends. If she needs an extra table for dinner, she simply makes one! The primitive barnboard table in her dining room has snagged many stockings and caused a few raised brows among more conservative dinner guests, but Melinda's goal is to create a setting where everyone feels relaxed. Skeptics are soon

won over by the sincere good wishes of the hostess, and by the unexpected dinners that she "stages," as opposed to "holds."

The nineteenth-century house, a former staff house for the now-defunct Black Hall School, is a small-scale version of many of the larger farmhouses that dot the surrounding Connecticut countryside. Despite its simplicity and modest proportions, Melinda's dining room aspires to grandeur, with gilded mirrors and frames, a tall screen draped with whatever fabric suits the mood and occasion, and other decorative accessories that might seem to be in conflict with her country tastes but somehow work effortlessly. "It's my version of faux formal," says Melinda, "or shabbily chic! I have eclectic tastes, and intend to have a good time decorating and entertaining."

Melinda learned to cook creatively with spices when she sailed the Mediterranean on a racing yacht, cooking for the crew and standing her share of watches. It was hurricane weather, and everyone looked forward to meals as respite from the elements and the hard work. Melinda's challenge was to tempt the sailors' appetites with deliciously spiced foods. She looks back fondly on her sailing days. Once, she said, "We played Bach for a whale who had fallen in love with our hull and was rocking it dangerously. Modern music would have capsized us. It was Bach who saved our lives and sent a contented whale swimming away."

Spontaneity is this hostess's muse; her travels are her inspiration. For Melinda, lighting serves to recreate a particular landscape in a room: "This effect can't be achieved with electricity, but only with color, texture, and candlelight, all of which play across a table, across a room, all night," she explains. "I want my guests to expect the unexpected." And, of course, they do.

The yard is "loaded" with poppies, according to Melinda, who clips them in the early morning hours to add color and cheer to a simple breakfast of yogurt and blueberries. Even the blue-and-white dish towels add a bright touch for sleepyheads. An impromptu table setting mixes things old and new: appealing pottery from a catalog; whimsical canine salt and pepper shakers; a yellowware bowl, always filled with fruit; and an old blue-and-white pitcher from Maine, greatly cherished despite its small scratches and chips.

Country pine night tables brought down from the guest room and covered with fine damask dinner napkins serve as a bar for a small dinner party. Melinda scavenges her local antiques shops to find mismatched sets of pretty hand-etched glasses that are beautiful both in price and in quality. To curb hungry appetites, a wheel of Brie has been set in hollowed-out peasant bread, decorated with triangles of almonds, dried cherries, walnuts, and dried basil, and baked till the cheese runs and the nuts brown slightly (recipe, p. 252).

Melinda has fun taking her dinner parties to obvious thematic extremes in her modest Connecticut farmhouse. For this particular group of friends, she's decided on a faux formal version of an evening in Venice, seen through the reflection of a gilded mirror. The glass-paneled screen is the perfect framework for touches of drama, in this instance peach moiré fabric, a thoughtful gift from a friend who knows Melinda's preferences for certain colors and textiles. An antique French satin fabric in gold and teal gently drapes across a primitive barnboard table, substituting for a tablecloth. Wicker chairs have been pressed into service from another room in the house.

A nine-teenth-century French cachepot becomes a vase for peonies from the garden. A pair of Italian candelabra, made of hand-wrought iron that has aged gracefully over many years, lights the setting. The antique dinnerware is Bavarian; the heavily embellished gold-plated flatware is a glamorous pattern with the plain name of Waldo. A salad of romaine lettuce and orange slices is colorful, simple, and delicious.

I

t's tea for one in the most comfortable chair in the house, a chance for Melinda to catch her breath before another busy evening.

Like a quick-change artist, Melinda can transform her dining room into many different charming and traditional settings. Here, silver accessory pieces combined with old English pottery set a new scene for a country luncheon. Embroidered place mats with elaborate cutwork cover the table. Two benches, made extra wide for comfort, flank the same barn-board table.

A miniature park bench by the California artist Susan Ryan, surrounded by tiny

The English pottery is Mason's Vista: "not the copy —it's the original!" adds Melinda. The salt cellars hold a coarse seasoned salt and chopped parsley is offered in a silver ashtray.

topiaries, creates a new
and different alternative to
a centerpiece.

Melinda admires the intri-
cate design and old-world
craftsmanship of these sil-
ver serving pieces — espe-
cially the plumes, beading,
and mother-of-pearl
ornamentation.

Petey, Melinda's parrot, prefers his lamp-shade perch to a gilded cage. Coffee will be served on this round corner table, dressed up with a white linen runner over a paisley cloth. Tokens of friendship and found objects—silver spurs from Mexico, a stone lion from Turkey, granite from a dig in Cairo—are remembrances of past journeys.

Melinda has sponge-painted inexpensive terra-cotta pedestals in green and dull gold, then set pillar candles on them, slipping leaves underneath. It's the season for peonies, a full and romantic flower that seems a perfect choice next to a cherub lamp.

Painted lawn chairs in the apple orchard provide repose.

Ice-cold daiquiris offer a break from the late-afternoon heat. The glass pitcher with its svelte lines holds enough for seconds, which are served in classic silver mint-julep cups originally from Kentucky.

DOWN HOME

The brightly painted entrance hall in the Gans family "farmhouse" where guests are greeted easily identifies the house as the work of the architect Robert A. M. Stern. Boldly arranged flowering cherry and apple blossoms are from the yard.

Every time Stephanie Gans throws a boardinghouse supper for family and friends, her guests feel like they're coming home to Granny's. An uprooted southerner, Stephanie says it makes her feel good to recreate these legendary suppers for Stephen, her "Yankee husband," and their teen-aged daughters, Alana and Sabrina. Stephanie's grand-mother, Minnie K., took in occasional boarders and was happy feeding a few—or a crowd. Almost intuitively, Stephanie now prepares all the "comfort foods" that she remembers from her child-hood in Georgia. Proper etiquette gives way at the Gans table to long reaches and elbow jabbing. No one says "Don't put so much on your plate." Or "Please pass the peas." That's just one reason why everyone loves a Minnie K. supper.

Stephanie Gans has a soft touch for anything with a homily on it, which partly explains her collection of samplers and English Devonshire pottery. These simple treasures remind Stephanie of her grand-mother, Minnie K., who would surely approve of this wise saying. No doubt Minnie K. would also ap-prove of this graceful and unaffected bouquet.

When this family of four makes up a joint guest list, it includes countless friends and friends' children, the generations mixing happily. The invitation can also be for a picnic or a buffet that can spill outdoors onto the lawn. "We have our regulars, who are affectionately called 'the cousins,'" says Stephanie, without question the chief organizer for such events. "That's a holdover from my childhood, when our family was large and we couldn't always remember just who was related and who wasn't, and it never really mattered."

Stephanie admits to a particular fondness for the old-fashioned variety stores where she picks up most of her party accessories and kitchen items. It pains her to see all the friendly old five-and-tens turning into gigantic and impersonal chains. Gingham tea towels on sale, vinyl-covered fabric in sweet floral patterns sold by the yard, green mason jars, and colorful tin canisters—these are among the pleasures at Stephanie's local dime store, which "hasn't changed since 1910." Imagination can turn a mayonnaise jar into a vase or a plain wooden stool into a pedestal.

Stephanie and Stephen think that eight is the perfect number for a sit-down dinner. These more formal occasions are times when children stay at home with baby-sitters, and often the sitters are the Gans daughters. The dining area of their generous living room has eight extremely comfortable upholstered chairs around an attractive country pine table. Stephanie does all the cooking and will often devote an entire day to preparing dinner.

The music is Stephen's bailiwick. A true aficionado, with eclectic taste, he'll gladly and correctly perform selections from a Buddy Holly album or identify some obscure popular or classical melody for anyone who has the courage to hum it. He'll spend hours sorting through the Ganses' extensive tape and CD collection to come up with an evening's mood music tailored to the style of a particular group. Stephen feels that people should spend more time selecting music for their parties, large or small.

With so much old-fashioned hospitality invested in every occasion, Stephanie and Stephen have a waiting list of "cousins" hoping for invitations.

"Granny would never fuss and put condiments in fancy containers. Everything went right on the table—plain and simple," recalls Stephanie.

Everyone wants to be invited to a "Minnie K." supper at Stephanie Gans's home, especially on a dull, rainy day. It's Stephanie's recreation of the boardinghouse spread she remembers from her childhood summers in Savannah, Georgia. Minnie K. was a warm and generous woman who took in occasional boarders and felt obliged to feed them well: southern fried chicken, black-eyed peas, Minnie K.'s Jell-O–Carrot Salad, Sweet Potatoes with Marshmallows (recipes, p. 252), collard greens, corn bread, vanilla-wafer pudding from a recipe on the box, and other customary southern foods. The boardinghouse style calls for oilcloth, plates and glasses turned over (to keep the flies off!), condiments right out of the jars, and generous portions meant to be reached for, not passed.

For a more formal occasion, a dining area of the spacious living room seats eight comfortably. Formal-style pine chairs have been upholstered in white duck. Two lace tablecloths meet in the center of the extra-long country pine table. Stephanie and Stephen sometimes prefer that their generous linen napkins be crisply starched and pressed. The dinnerware is a reproduction of Blue Willow; here it shows off the Cold Beet Soup (recipe, p. 253).

Since the mood of this dinner is Victorian, Stephanie has created place cards by affixing old-fashioned stickers to plain cards that rest on small easels. Pretty wired French ribbon holds its shape and adds a decorative touch to the English turned-wood candle holder. Abundant fresh-cut lilacs, arranged in a pedestal fruit dish, add to the romantic mood. The flowers are held in place with florist's tape and Oasis. A small bird's nest and a rabbit dish are un-expected touches.

Rose~Lee

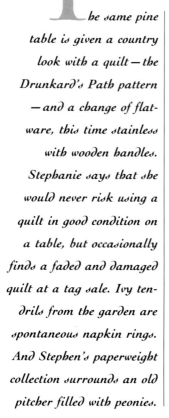

*T*he same pine table is given a country look with a quilt—the Drunkard's Path pattern —and a change of flatware, this time stainless with wooden handles. Stephanie says that she would never risk using a quilt in good condition on a table, but occasionally finds a faded and damaged quilt at a tag sale. Ivy tendrils from the garden are spontaneous napkin rings. And Stephen's paperweight collection surrounds an old pitcher filled with peonies.

By sunlight or by candle-
light, the beauty and mystery of the paperweights
steal the show. "Everyone
wants to hold them," says
Stephen, who looks for ad-
ditions to his collection on
business trips as a break
from his work routine. "At
dinner parties, they never
end up in the places where
they started."

Antique perfume bottles
sometimes double as
charming small vases, and
the whole collection makes
an effective and unusual
table arrangement.

These hosts believe that guests are ready for more relaxed seating at the dessert course. Strawberry shortcake is served buffet style from the sofa table, a pretty vintage lace bedspread serving as a cloth. Stephanie has clipped apple blossoms from a tree in the yard for the table. The pot of ivy is borrowed from another room. There is never a shortage of comfortable seating space in this gracious living room, where guests are happy to linger long after coffee.

E ven a paint-spattered bench just outside a screened-in porch receives a bit of adornment in the form of a daisy topiary. It can be appreciated by passersby and also seen by guests from within.

G uests with young children appreciate Stephanie's attention to their needs. A textile designer before her two daughters were born, Stephanie believes that children appreciate color and design. Here, she has added a bright vintage tablecloth to a picnic table set just for children, and has even given them their own flower arrangement.

An extra door found in the garage has been covered in vinyl-coated fabric available by the yard. The makeshift picnic table sits on wooden planters. Inexpensive dish towels are good for wiping sticky hands and mopping up spills. Baskets hold snacks and juice. It's fun for the children to discover their places by searching for the right paper plate.

Al Fresco

The eat-in kitchen at Amanda and Lewis Berman's weekend cottage is a friendly gathering place where guests can offer a hand or just pull up a chair. A simple lettuce, tomato, and cucumber sandwich becomes a pretty still life on slices of still-warm bread. Mizuna from the garden is peppery in taste and spiky in appearance, an interesting garnish for sandwiches and many main dishes.

Many travelers pack excess clothes when they go on vacation. The Bermans are more likely to pack good wine, cooking equipment, and the ingredients of some new recipe that Amanda—an assistant at a New York cooking school—plans to try at leisure. Once, a pound bag of French green lentils checked through in a suitcase split open en route. "We still haven't seen the end of them!" says Lewis. On another plane trip, Amanda's knives—the tools of the trade for any professional cook—were confiscated by airport security as "dangerous weapons." Their daughters,

Meredith and Michelle, have been known to travel with the family's two Jack Russell terriers in one carry bag and a gourmet lunch in another.

Travel adventures with essential paraphernalia are simpler when Lewis and Amanda pack the car on Fridays and head for their second home—a shingled cottage on eastern Long Island. The house was originally a tractor shed and storage area for a potato harvest from the surrounding fields. During the fifties, previous owners turned the shed into a house—"a knotty-pine heaven." The Bermans wasted no time modernizing the interior and adding a convenient eat-in kitchen, mostly for Amanda.

Curiosity about makeshift signs and arrows on their country road led Lewis and Amanda to a garage sale where a serendipitous find was a set of four sturdy and handsome old ladderback chairs. The good English pine table forgives occasional nicks, scratches, and water marks. The antique wire pedestal basket is just the right size and shape for a centerpiece of cherries—meant for admiration and dessert.

On another day, lunch goes alfresco when a picnic's in the making. Tasty sandwich fillings — Curried Egg Salad and Tempting Tuna Salad (recipes, p. 253) — along with a traditional favorite, Waldorf salad, are ready and waiting on the kitchen table. Sandwiches and other picnic fare will be packed in wicker hampers and carried to a spot on the lawn.

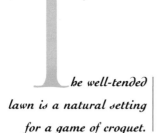

The well-tended lawn is a natural setting for a game of croquet.

Amanda doesn't cook; she conjures a meal with such cheerful spontaneity that visitors to her kitchen rarely suspect the effort. "You could have gone to a restaurant and it wouldn't have tasted as good," says Lewis, who is generous with his praise. As for Lewis's role: "I just let him talk," says Amanda with equal affection. "Lewis is such a wonderful conversationalist that it leaves me free to concentrate on the table and the meal." Lewis is also a New York veterinarian, once called "the Jet Set's Pet Vet" by a national magazine, a nickname that has stuck. Visitors' dogs and cats are always welcome, and pet stories are legion at parties.

When the weather turns warm, entertaining goes outdoors to a wide lawn that runs the length of a football field, beginning at the modest cottage and ending at a tall privet hedge. In between is the Bermans' interpretation of an English garden, white admiral phlox, monarda, and nicotiana punctuated by bright yellow coreopsis. The Bermans know that their lawn and garden are overdeveloped for the site, but, for them, it is a matter of priorities. "We are devoted to our gardening," states Amanda, "and we like to share it with our friends." Sharing means a croquet picnic with a flower bed as a backdrop, a buffet dinner under the sheltering linden tree, or a merry romp for dogs delighted with so much green.

Amanda keeps an entertaining diary, which she fills with menus, guest lists, the names of people's pets, and comments about the occasion. It would be difficult to imagine a bad review when good things come together in such harmony.

S urrounded by | the modest shingled cottage
potato fields on two sides | boasts a lawn and gardens
and a twenty-five-foot | that far grander homes
privet hedge on the others, | would envy.

*"I carried my grandmoth-
er's garden basket on my
lap all the way back to
New York from Sussex,"
remembers Amanda, who
believes she actually inher-
ited her love of gardening
from her American father.
Her English grandmother
would surely have approved
of the exquisite mix of hydrangeas in the split-wood
trug that once held her
cherished garden tools.*

*Following pages: The full-
ness of the flowers and the
intensity of their colors
make an irresistible setting
for the picnic. A square of
sisal has been transformed
into an artist's canvas by
Andre LaPorte, a local artisan. Attractive old wicker
hampers are always practical for transporting lunch.*

*J*ust so the sandwiches aren't a mystery, Amanda has placed decoratively labeled gift stickers on each of them. The English hamper came outfitted with plastic plates and a full set of flatware. The original cup holders are handy for salt, pepper, and other small picnic necessities.

To add a touch of celebra-
tion and keep the bugs
away, Amanda has
wrapped her Sweet Finale
Toffee Bars (recipe, p.
253) in tinted cellophane,
then tied them with colorful
gift ribbon. A mason jar,
chilled in the refrigerator
all morning, holds plenty
of lemonade.

Moving the kitchen table and chairs into the garden under the sheltering linden tree is worth the effort. "Everyone appreciates an early supper when that magical late-afternoon breeze begins," says Lewis.

"It's a time for Amanda and me to show off the garden when the sun is low and the shadows are soft." Amanda has cut dozens of snapdragons for a full and romantic arrangement in a large spongeware bowl.

It's a true country buffet when the food is presented in an old wheelbarrow filled with fresh straw. An assistant at a French cooking school, Amanda tailors her cooking to the occasion —be it a deliciously basic menu or one that demands a professional's skill. Tonight the fare for good friends is uncomplicated: Chicken Salad with Grapes, pickled beets from the garden, and green salad with Special Salad Dressing (recipe, p. 254).

A gigantic leaf-shaped place mat, set here on an oversized paper doily, is certainly appropriate. Pansy-decorated dessert plates, a gift from Amanda's parents, are placed on rose-colored service plates and further echo the garden theme. Light, sweet, and topped with berries in season, lemon tarts are one of Lewis and Amanda's favorite desserts.

The hungry picnickers — Maude (the most eager!), Lily and Daisy (canine hosts), Lew (no relation to the human host!), Foster (recently adopted and getting used to the good life), and Chester (a dog with good connections) — are on their best behavior while waiting for Amanda's Doggie Treats (recipe, p. 254).

Lewis, a veterinarian, says
their family is fond of
Jack Russell terriers be-
cause "they're short like we
are!" One might also add
"amusing" and "intelli-
gent." Lily and Daisy are
dressed up because it's their
turn to have friends over.

COUNTRY INFLUENCES

"We rarely took the ice bucket out of the cupboard," said Margo Ravon of the silver bucket shaped like a top hat, "until we discovered it was more useful—and certainly more whimsical—when used for flowers." The cleomes and white cosmos are from one of Margo's garden beds.

When the Ravons moved into their new home, a converted nineteenth-century barn, relatives from as far away as France came to visit, bearing housewarming gifts and hearty good wishes. Naturally, everyone was eager to see how Margo and Jean-Michel had turned a horse barn—its timber bearing a century's worth of grime and stable grit—into a gracious home for their young family of four. It was fortunate that the barn's former owner was in the landscaping business, for the property had thick, lush lawns worthy of an estate, with well-pruned trees and a scattering of flowering bushes. But the barn itself lay untouched, challenging the Ravons to make it their own while retaining its historical integrity.

The barn is now an attractive and airy home for Margo, Jean-Michel, and their two young daughters, Lauren and Perri. As new home owners, the Ravons furnished and accessorized the house from scratch. They agreed on keeping their entertaining simple, preferring to spend free time cooking and gardening, sharing the work and the praise. Margo and Jean-Michel think it's smart to rely on the basics: a set of white china, attractive but practical glassware, and twelve place settings of wood-handled flatware brought back from France. Margo treasures the handcrafted serving pieces she finds at craft shows: she enjoys buying directly from artisans, feeling more connected to the piece and to the artist who made it.

Margo and Jean-Michel Ravon had a special vision when they purchased an original nineteenth-century barn—straw and all—on a rolling two-acre parcel several years ago. Naturally, friends and family members, many from France, which is Jean-Michel's home, were eager to visit the completed house. The original barn doors are now the entrance.

A *new
picket fence surrounds the
combination vegetable/
flower garden and adjoins
an old outbuilding that was
once a henhouse.*

A miniature garden close to the house was inspired by photographs and memories of grander, more formal gardens in England and France. The center of the garden's design is decorative brickwork laid in a circle, with brick paths separating the beds and leading to the edges in a radial design. Jean-Michel accomplished the bricklaying; he and Margo later constructed a charming picket fence from unfinished pine, which weathers well. Their very first growing season resulted in a forest of leaf lettuce, enough basil for many pesto sauces, and a bumper crop of zucchini and tomatoes. The garden in season provides food and flowers for the table.

The Ravons were rewarded by a magnificent lettuce crop at the end of their very first year of gardening efforts.

A meandering stone wall was a joint effort by the fathers of Margo and Jean-Michel, one a Frenchman and the other an American. Built from local river rock, it appears to have been there for centuries. The height makes it perfect for a summer buffet.

A long-running off-Broadway play, *The Fantasticks*, tells of two fathers who build a wall to keep their son and daughter apart. The Ravons' story is a complete reversal. Their respective fathers—one from Massachusetts and the other from France—collaborated on the building of a stone wall on the west side of the property near the house. The wall, constructed of local river rock, meanders along a grassy embankment and appears to have been there for centuries. It's the perfect height for children to use as a pretend balance beam or just to sit on and dangle their legs. A yearly American-style celebration of Bastille Day takes place by the wall, with bowls of delicious cold salads and baskets of warm country breads. Two cultures blend easily in this home.

A weathered copper cooking pot is turned into a serving vessel for a Northern White Bean Salad (recipe, p. 255), one of several delicious salads.

*T*he simply adorned farm-stand basket was given a good rinsing before being filled with lettuce and nasturtiums from the garden—more than enough to go around. A picnic hamper holds the bread—French baguettes, of course.

An old berry carrier makes a perfect tray for chubby Spirited Chocolate Chip Cookies and Moist Applesauce Chunkies, filled with raisins and bits of dried apricot (recipes, p. 255).

Cold drinks taste even bet- | simple to turn glasses up-
ter on a hot day if the | side down in their own
glasses are frosted. It's | basket of ice.

A handsome kitchen with a convenient work space now occupies the former stable area. Margo and Jean-Michel often cook with their young daughters — Lauren and Perri — and pizza-making is always a favorite activity.

Although this pizza party is not for kids only, it's certainly tailored to their likes and needs. Heavy brown paper covers the table and turns it into an enormous drawing board. An ample supply of crayons is important so that no one fights over their favorite colors. A brown grocery bag, crushed down to form a bowl, makes a disposable serving vessel for grapes.

P erri and Lauren
have signed their artwork.

There is nothing breakable
about this party. Late-
nineteenth-century spatter-
painted graniteware, a relative of tinware, is light
weight and durable.
Painting a coffee can turns
it into a vase for zinnias.

*S*eashells col-
lected at a local beach and
arranged on the sill make
a decorative window
dressing.

It doesn't take advance planning to invite a friend for tea, which can be savored in these comfortable antique wicker chairs. The 1920s German teapot is made of hammered silver and was Margo's gift to herself on what she describes as a "Mommy Get-Away Trip." Fine damask that was purchased in France by the roll was later made into both napkins and guest towels for the powder room.

The Ravons have begun to collect contemporary folk art, which fits comfortably into their rustic yet sophisticated setting. Here, wooden birds by the folk artist Daniel Hale circle a leafy nest on a pine table.

A single sunflower in an earthenware bowl is more dramatic than a full bouquet.

*A*frican violets sit sweetly on rockers made from wooden clothes pins by Les Jones, whose handiwork is always on display at the Jones family's produce stand during the summer.

An arrangement in a wine carrier gives the appearance of a flower bed, with four colors of freesia placed in drinking glasses and settled in openings designed for bottles.

Hospitality longer than a country mile draws repeat guests to the northwest Connecticut home of long-time antiques dealers Evan Hughes and Peter Erma-cora. Their welded and painted horseshoe chair, part of a complete set, is easily identified as English from the shape of the horse's shoes. A blueberry pie awaits weekend guests.

Only a first-time visitor would go to the front door of Evan G. Hughes and Peter Ermacora's eighteenth-century home. Everyone else walks around to the more familiar kitchen door—the one that squeaks open and bangs shut with predictable frequency. A latched door means nothing in this part of Connecticut—still genuine farm country reminiscent of the Cotswolds—where friends and neighbors rarely wait for an official invitation to pay a call. Even the house cat comes and goes at leisure; a long stretch to the latch, and she's halfway across the open field.

With the old cow barn in back of the house now turned into a storage hold for many of their tasteful acquisitions, including this charming gar-den bench, these hosts rarely worry about extra chairs for a standing-room-size crowd.

It's just this sort of ease and quality of life that Evan and Peter were seeking when they abandoned an overcommitted city life five years ago. For seventeen years, Evan had been a successful florist, designing other people's parties with panache while woefully neglecting his own. With Peter as his partner in an antiques business, E.G.H. Peter ("It has the same rhythm as F.A.O. Schwarz!"), they began to combine flowers with fine country furniture and sell both at a downtown New York shop. Their unerring taste and approachable style soon won them a faithful clientele.

When Evan and Peter moved to the country, they set up a furniture gallery in their home and hoped that clients and friends would follow, which they did—quite literally. "We'll pick you up at the diner," Peter tells guests who travel by public transportation. At the diner, the only one in town, there's no mistaking their frazzled city

S pongeware old (the bowl) and spongeware new (the plates and bread dish) — only a few of many pieces from an impressive spongeware collection — mix successfully. A late-summer picnic menu includes Evan's E.G.H. Pasta specialty, made with ripe local tomatoes, and Peter's warm Easy Rosemary Focaccia (recipes, p. 256).

"Our city guests arrive on the Saturday morning train in need of clean air, sunshine, green grass, and a view," says Evan, who provides all that and an alfresco lunch to begin the visit. A portable picnic

visitors. When guests arrive at the house, they might assume that Evan is back in the flower business, for this early riser usually spends the dawn hours in the woods gathering vines, tree branches, berries, and wildflowers. A jungle of bittersweet in a redware jug, punctuated with dozens of stems of Queen Anne's lace, says it all. Evan's advice about arrangements, which he happily offers, is simple: "Don't run out to buy it before you look first in your own backyard, and don't get all worked up over how it will look. How could flowers look bad?"

During the weekend, the entertaining will move from place to place—indoors and out. The corn is high and there's shade by the barn, so out comes a portable picnic table and a stack of spongeware plates. It's a trek from the kitchen to the barn, so guests form a procession

table dating back "a few years" can be brought close enough to the field to hear the corn rustling. Homer, Bart, and Sara are curious visitors from the neighboring farm.

This household's motto is "We fix the first drink; the rest are self-serve." Guests gather around a bar set up on a drop-leaf maple table in the keeping room. Popcorn is a household trademark, and friends anticipate it salted, buttered, and in good supply. Everyone always stops to admire the early Ameri-

bearing the food and the accoutrements for a picnic at midday. Saturday also means a cocktail party with substantial hors d'oeuvres and an endless supply of salted popcorn, which is standard fare here. The kitchen expands into a large keeping room, and everyone tends to congregate in that room. To keep the crowd flowing throughout, various foods are set out in every room. "Put the shrimp where you want people to go," is Evan and Peter's advice.

Everyone stays on, knowing from previous occasions that a board game will be pulled from a cupboard or that someone will rearrange the chairs for a hilarious game of charades or even a magic show. "Games keep parties from getting stuffy," the hosts suggest. And at spontaneous good times like these, the word "stuffy" simply has no place.

can hooked rug mounted, like a painting, on a canvas stretcher. The armchair on the left is a rare form—a cast-metal chair in a Windsor design intended for garden use. The ribbon-back design on the side chair adds a formal note to a painted country style dating to 1830.

American crystal decanters, well-executed copies of an older design, were borrowed from Peter's sister, who lives nearby, for one of Hughes and Ermacora's signature open-house cocktail parties. Decanters are an attractive way to offer a variety of spirits. Evan was the first New York florist to introduce wildflowers as a "look" to sophisticated city customers, who were stuck in a hothouse rut. His fresh and unstructured arrangements are legendary.

To move guests along from room to room and avoid a bottleneck, Peter has tried-and-true advice: "People will go where the shrimp is." So a basket of shrimp is set on a handmade veneered bark table in the living room under a rare sign dated 1847. The sign, painted on both sides, was discovered in its original curlicued frame in the attic of an old Vermont store.

A treasured Black Hawk weather vane, made by Harris & Co. of Boston during the late nineteenth century, appears to gallop on a forest of ivy and juniper branches. Jumbo shrimp, bought cleaned and cooked, fill a glass bowl set in a new rustic basket.

Following pages: Under the watchful eye of folk artist Zedekiah Belknap's Portrait of a Gentleman—dated circa 1830—guests make their way into the dining room, where a sawbuck table holds an unrestrained arrangement of bittersweet, viburnum, hydrangeas, and Queen Anne's lace. Two pairs of antique candle holders cast soft light over the room even in daylight. "There's no rule that says candles can only be lighted when it's pitch black," say the home owners.

The fruit looks inviting, but beware!—it's antique American stone! English ironstone embellished with the copper luster pattern known as Tea Leaf found favor in the White House dining room during the Lincoln administration. Evan and Peter's extensive collection includes a covered berry bowl and small relish dishes.

The local vegetable stand offers a wealth of fresh garden vegetables, including miniature red and yellow tomatoes, baby squash, and snap peas. When selecting vegetables for crudités, the hosts pay attention to color.

*T*his splendid vinegar-painted tiger maple cupboard contains a sample of the dealers' early redware collection. "The irony of painted tiger maple," Peter explains, "is that people once painted inexpensive woods to look like more exotic, expensive varieties. Today, because of the rarity of these fantasy pieces, their prices far exceed those made from the finer woods."

An open cupboard is a good place to show off collections. Displayed here is both American and English pewter, Canton china, an anonymous folk-art painting, handsome lead crystal glasses, and a gilded wooden quill — an early Odd Fellows symbol now mounted for display.

*New furniture in an old
Adirondack design, looking
fresh and sculptural on the
veranda, invites guests to
slide back and relax over a
dessert of fruit and sherry.*

*The secret of this fruit sal-
ad's mosaic design is the
way Peter layers grapes,
strawberries, nectarines,
plums, peaches, mandarin
orange slices (the only
canned ingredient), blue-
berries, and two kinds of
melon balls — cantaloupe
and honeydew.*

E legant dam-
ask napkins and delicate
etched glasses filled with
fine sherry bring a week-
end in the country to a
satisfying conclusion.

Weekend

Company

GRACIOUS HOSPITALITY

An avid gardener, Diane Fisher fills waiting metal buckets with seasonal flowers for her charming beachside cottage.

Weekend guests are content to be second in importance to Diane Fisher's garden, and they are accustomed to finding her on her knees when they arrive, weeding the hollyhocks, pruning the roses, or cutting foxgloves for the luncheon table. An elegant series of plantings modeled after the great estate gardens of Europe but reduced in proportion to the half-acre lot, Diane's garden winds around her Long Island, New York, beach cottage and meanders as if by nature's whimsy into the yard beyond. It enhances the welcoming feeling about the small house, where guests find cool lemonade set out during the day and soft antique quilts for their beds at night.

Freshly cut cosmos and miniature gladiolus sit in a stoneware crock, waiting to be arranged.

"I spend a lot of time cooking and even more doing the flowers and the table," says Diane, who has enough suggestions to write her own entertaining book. Delightful touches throughout the house include Diane's "English garden arrangements" in unusual flower containers—old inkwells, milk pails, custard cups, and small fruit crates. Arrangements are accented with found objects and bits of nature: smooth beach pebbles, birds' nests, twigs, beach grass, and colorful shards of glass or china. Diane describes the country atmosphere as "casual,

Lemonade and cookies on the back porch provide a welcome break. The cotton cushions and tablecloth on the antique wicker rocker and side chair have a pleasing sun-bleached look, which tells guests that bare feet on the outdoor furniture are permissible.

cluttered, and eclectic." One could certainly add "grace-ful, innovative, and tasteful."

Years ago, a guest admired the table linens that Diane had made—appealing blue-and-white napkins edged in white lace—and suggested she turn her natural talent into a business. Eager for a career change and more independence, she took this advice. Now, Diane Fisher designs and distributes table linens nationally for a New York company, and her home is often a testing ground for new ideas.

It follows that Diane's tables are special—frequently dressed for company with layers of pretty linens both new and old. "People get stuck doing the same old things over and over," laments this hostess, who regularly changes her own style with fresh ideas. She'll toss a quilt, an Indian rug, or a tartan wool blanket over a bare table, then find napkins to match. If she can't find the right napkins, she'll design and make them. "I wasn't born with a special gene for tabletop design. There's simply a personal satisfaction for me in creating a warm and in-viting atmosphere at my table."

A long shelf in the kitchen is devoted to favorite cook-books that are dog-eared at the most successful recipes. Diane's meals consist of tried-and-true dishes that have gone over well in the past. She prefers to experiment at leisure for a good friend or two before unveiling a dish at a larger gathering.

There's no last-minute shopping or running out of Dijon mustard or olive oil for this organized hostess. Diane's pantry is always well stocked with all the basics:

An old lamp-shade frame has been recovered with a delicate netting fabric, then decorated with a vintage fruit adornment and bows of French ribbon, to form a foil for uninvited flying visitors. Old-fashioned Lemon-Almond Sugar Cookies (recipe, p. 257) are piled beneath the cover.

Y ou can pucker up or go sweet, since the lemonade is the do-it-yourself kind, inspired by the European tradition of setting out fresh lemon juice and a pitcher of sugar syrup with plenty of mint leaves and ice.

seasonings, spices, candles, flower containers, liquors, and freshly pressed linens. (See "Diane's Suggestions for a Well-Stocked Pantry," page 267.) The closets in her cottage are few and small, so she makes up for the lack of space by organizing table linens by color, with cloths and napkins stacked together. "If you can't see it, you don't use it."

A stereo is tucked out of sight in a cupboard, with the evening's tapes and CDs stacked in an order that the hostess has planned. Despite Diane's attention to detail, she readily admits that "Sometimes the most special evenings just can't be planned." But when the flowers begin to scent every room and the hearty aroma from the kitchen wafts through the open doors, it's difficult to believe that Diane's meticulous planning won't pay off.

Through an outside porch window, visitors can see the full, blossoming hydrangea tree beyond. When fall arrives and the tree is cut back for the winter, guests always depart with an armful of glorious blooms to take home to dry.

The paintings of Claude
Monet became the inspira-
tion and theme for this table setting. The rich blues
and golden yellows of the

Diane's linen drawers are
filled with the wares of her
trade, providing a new look
for every occasion. She prefers tablecloths that brush
the floor and likes to tie the
corners bandanna style.

*French provincial-style
placemats and napkins
play against the paleness
of the vintage cloth placed
atop a second tablecloth.*

*Bright sunflowers nearly
topple their tiny glass
vases. A deep casserole by
the ceramicist Barbara Eigen in blue and yellow becomes the centerpiece. Place
cards containing a variety
of fruit motifs may be
erased and used again.*

I t's easy to see why
Diane is attracted to the
palette of the French
Impressionists. Soft yellows
with bright accents of blues
and greens are a recurrent
color theme in the dining
room. And when her garden
is in full bloom, Diane cuts
flowers for every room.

The same chest of drawers that holds extra linens also serves as a buffet for a simple meal. The Asparagus-Stuffed Chicken Breasts with Prosciutto and Goat Cheese (recipe, p. 257) may be served at room temperature with a simple pasta. Practical wooden utensils are at the ready for weekend guests, who are happy to serve themselves in this setting.

With a full house and a busy Monday on the horizon, Diane looks for simple, delicious desserts. It's hard to beat fresh peaches and whipped cream with raspberry sauce on the side. The gravy boat, part of Diane's antique blueware collection, serves the dessert sauce. The useful bowls are from her collection of old kitchenware.

he rose arbor, where guests may wander during the brief but breath-taking blooming period, is the perfect setting for tea. Diane fills her table with traditional English sweets —scones and lemon tarts —plus an American favorite, the decadent brownie.

Diane's penchant for lemon motifs can be seen in her new creamer and sugar bowl as well as in her old sugar shaker. The Arts and Crafts teapot keeps close company with a new needlework tea cozy. The differing heights of the cut-glass serving plates give variety and order to the table arrangement, which might otherwise seem flat and crowded.

Delicate and rare, many of the varieties of roses in Diane's arbor can be traced back to eighteenth-century France. The elegant names —Duchess of Montebello, Comte de Chambord, and Juno—recall French history. Blue glassware from the 1940s was once a popular giveaway in movie theaters and grocery stores.

D iane has brought out a hat appro- priate to the occasion.

A translucent glow from the blue glass plates makes them a pretty choice for these delicate pastries. Cot- ton lace napkins are the perfect choice from Diane's linen closet.

A majolica pitcher holds
roses from the arbor,
awaiting a place of honor
in the cottage.

A Chef in the Family

Eban Ross, son of home owners Joanna and Howard Ross, is the expert chef in this family. At the Rosses' weekend home, he works on this natural butcher-block cutting board, with fresh vegetables, raw tuna from the local fish farm, and a brand-new set of stainless-steel knives, tools of the trade for Eban.

Joanna and Howard Ross are living a parental fantasy: to be rewarded in kind for the countless meals they prepared over the years for their children. Their sons each used to claim that it was the other's turn to help with the dishes. Now Adam—a waiter by night and an MFA candidate by day—does the serving, bartending, and clean-up for brother Eban, a recent graduate of the French Culinary Institute in New York.

Family weekends together at Joanna and Howard's country home nestled among pine trees give Eban a chance to experiment with food combinations for a supportive group of critics, who inevitably steer the conversation to food. Eban talks about the summer he spent as an exchange student in rural France, living with a family whose delicious and informal meals inspired him to pursue cooking as a career. "They sent me to the garden for rosemary," he relates, "but all I found were these enormous yew bushes, like the ones just off our porch back home. Well, those bushes *were* the rosemary! And ever since I clipped those herbs for dinner, I've never forgotten the sweet aroma and the way it lasted on my hands."

"It's such a pleasure to have Eban cooking for us, and in such an elaborate and tasteful way," says Joanna, a ballet teacher and personal fitness trainer. Howard Ross, an actor whose career has included starring roles in *Jacques Brel*, *Oliver!*, and *The Rothschilds*, says the only role left

The Rosses (as much as I'd like to, I can't claim these Rosses as relatives!) wanted their second home—postmodern in style—to be filled with serene light even on the dreariest day and to handle a steady flow of guests with ease. Eban and his brother, Adam, need no prompting to visit on weekends, with a good-natured retinue of friends always in tow.

for him at parties is making his famous strawberry margaritas.

Their postmodern house is filled with light, even when the weather is gloomy, thanks to white-stained floors, cream-colored walls, and an abundance of windows. Tastefully decorated rooms are filled with romantic floral

fabrics, softly worn antique rag rugs, and the family possessions that Joanna treasures. Two antique hurricane lamps, the glass delicately etched, occupy a prominent spot on a built-in buffet. Her mother's cerulean blue-glazed Mexican pottery brings back memories of casual entertaining when Joanna was growing up. It now fills their cupboards and decorates several walls. Eban has developed a special appreciation for these everyday heirlooms: "I feel that the history of my family and that of the plates brings out the sincerity in my cooking."

The kitchen occupies a large portion of the downstairs living area and contains a center island with high stools on one side—the favorite gathering spot. Sunday morning is a time to have friends over. Brunch becomes lunch, thanks to the late hours of the college-age crowd. It's also a more elaborate spread than most, thanks to Eban, who always begins his brunches with hors d'oeuvres. "Why not? It's good to break the rules," he says. "After all, cold fruit soup is really just a way for adults to have dessert first."

A round table seats eight comfortably. "We managed twelve once," added Adam, "but then no one could move their elbows to eat!" Since cloths for a table so large are difficult to find, Joanna purchased a cotton sheet — the pattern an elegant allover brocade — and had it made into a tablecloth with napkins to match. Striking black ladder-back chairs — well-constructed reproductions — stand out against the soothing cream-colored walls, accenting an artistically spare and graceful table setting that reflects the tastes of Joanna, a former ballet dancer, and Howard, an actor.

ouquets of dried flowers and herbs have been fastened to every chair back with strands of raffia. After brunch, the flowers will be gathered together and placed in the guest room.

Joanna says the tiny chips in her unusual cream-and-blue Mexican dinnerware are part of the pottery's character, a part of its history. She recalls happy times during her childhood when her mother would set a table with this same dinnerware. The service for sixteen has survived many moves and many festive occasions. Several plates, hung as decoration, occupy permanent spots on the walls. The sterling flatware was Joanna's mother's wedding silver, and is yet another treasured heirloom.

A hand-crafted twig basket makes a wonderful rustic container for flowers when lined first with moss and then filled wtih water-soaked Oasis. A combination of daisies, miniature daisies, peach-colored mums, and blue trumpet flowers adds a springlike touch to the table.

Food is foremost now in Eban's life. He waxes eloquent about the produce at the farm stand that day, or the freshness of the local fish. "I find that most people worry so much about what's proper that the plate becomes nothing more than a rote repetition of a page out of a cookbook," he says, which is why Eban begins his meals creatively, on paper, with a sketch-pad drawing of the plated meal. He pays careful attention to color, texture, and the proportion of elements—details that mortal cooks rarely take to such professional extremes. "For me, food is an expression of caring, so the smiles on the faces of my family and our guests give me enormous satisfaction." And the critics agree.

Eban has created so many flavored butters (recipes, p. 257) that guests are usually treated to a variety, including Black Olive, Mixed Herbs, Cracked Black Pepper, and Garlic.

*N*ot every-one serves hors d'oeuvres at brunch, but here, Eban has prepared Spicy Tuna Tar-tare, Roquefort-Yogurt Puree en Endive, and Lemon Shrimp (recipes, p. 258). Cotton place mats are used under the serving pieces; the hurricane lamps are family heirlooms. An old copper bucket holds champagne.

Everyone's been waiting for the Smoked Salmon and Leek Frittata (recipe, p. 259). Eban prefers to pre-pare frittatas in individual ramekins when cooking for a crowd. These are flavored with fresh chives and tasty bits of salmon.

When setting her table, Joanna has trouble choosing between the cream-and-blue Mexican dinnerware and this second set, a cheerful floral pattern. The loosely woven Mexican napkin is part of a set that was purchased for use with both patterns. A Scandinavian rag rug protects the tabletop.

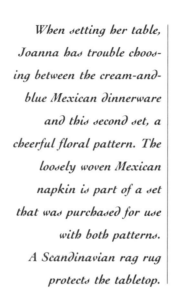

Eban is always conscious of the colors of a meal and how food looks on the plate. The balance here pleases the chef: bright steamed julienned zucchini, yellow squash, and carrots; slices of roasted new potatoes; a simple relish of chopped tomatoes and Bermuda onions; and the frittata resting on a bed of lettuce. Blue-rimmed wine-glasses, a holiday gift from Eban to his parents, harmonize with the other blues on the table.

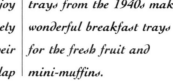

Joanna and Howard enjoy being served a leisurely breakfast in bed by their son. Prettily painted lap trays from the 1940s make wonderful breakfast trays for the fresh fruit and mini-muffins.

olly has trouble minding her manners when a pitcher of milk is so close by. The wallpaper-covered bandbox in the bedroom echoes the wonderful flowers found throughout the house and garden. The grand-style chair was a studio prop, acquired by the actor of the family for the master bedroom.

DESIGNING WAYS

The fabric and wall-covering samples that spill from Susan Lyle's tote bag are not intended for her; neither are the dining chairs she recently purchased. Susan has been an interior designer for fourteen years; her expertise ranges from total renovations to selecting tabletop accessories.

Susan Lyle and her husband, Clint Rodenberg, enjoy preparing for a casual "at home" at their Connecticut country house. Clint has set out a fruit and cheese arrangement in a wooden tray. Stacks of old books make decorative pedestals for plates and napkins. On the mantel are a tin trompe l'oeil vase, two fabric clowns, and a row of ceramic fruit echoed in the still-life by Robert Kulicke.

Her clients, many of whom have become good friends, sing her praises: "Susan's way is gentle, never imposing. She just makes my taste look better!"

While Susan's overall color sense tends toward more mellow hues—soft yellows, roses, and delicate greens pleasingly mixed with a deep nineteenth-century palette—she will

frequently add a surprising punch of Caribbean color— a hot pink or a flashy turquoise. "Decorators and clients alike can get stuck in a rut and forget to have fun with new color combinations," she says.

For Susan, setting a table means experimenting on a small scale. Since it doesn't involve buying fifty rolls of nonreturnable wallpaper or painting a house, if the new napkin colors scream "No!" she can simply return them. The way Susan presents her table, with slightly unexpected touches and impeccable taste, demonstrates her total approach to design and living. With so much thoughtful energy invested in other people's homes,

As the oldest of nine grandchildren, Susan developed a special relationship with her grandmother, whose splendid hurricane lamps she now owns. A wheel of pungent blue cheese and a large wedge of parmesan fill the serving board. "Tiny portions of lots of cheeses look stingy and indecisive," comments Clint. "I generally buy large chunks of a few good cheeses."

C lint, a wines and spirits executive, does most of the shopping and cooking while Susan, a designer, prefers to focus on the tabletop. Not one to be cautious with color, Susan was attracted to the striking colors of dinner plates by the ceramicist Lyn Evans. For country entertaining, she plays up the hot colors in the design. The bright pink and melon are repeated in an abstractly painted napkin, as well as on a bright straw mat placed on top of a handwoven rug by Sara Hotchkiss. By pairing the same plates with a more monochromatic color scheme, Susan sometimes changes the mood completely for formal entertaining back in the city.

everyone wonders where Susan finds time for her own.

Having a husband who shares the responsibilities is certainly an advantage, and Clint Rodenberg, according to Susan, does so admirably. It came as no surprise to Susan that Clint, a graduate of Cornell University's School of Hotel Administration, is thoroughly at home in the role of host. Their first meeting was at a dinner party at Clint's bachelor apartment nearly nineteen years ago. This was during the early seventies, when men eager to impress had to struggle just to translate a French menu, but Clint already knew how to prepare one. "She fell for my chocolate soufflé," he muses. To this day, Clint, a senior vice president for a wines and spirits importer,

When the weather grows chilly, glass panels replace the window screens in this multifunction porch, in use year round. Woven leather chairs and a pine table designed by the local cabinet-makers James Dew & Son create an attractive dining area. A platter of smoked fish garnished with rosemary and another of cold asparagus vinaigrette await afternoon guests.

does most of the cooking and the shopping, while Susan admits she is "a foreigner in a grocery store."

Their country home is a 1940s ranch-style bungalow, imaginatively renovated to include an updated eat-in kitchen. Weekends away from the city afford Clint long, leisurely days to do most of the cooking, whether it's for Susan and their teenage daughter, Lyle, or for a number of guests. Just steps away is a large screened-in porch, the windows of which can be fitted with removable glass panels during the cooler months, giving the family another year-round room for entertaining. With its open-air feeling and a panoramic view of the yard and the pool, the porch is inevitably where everyone gathers.

On the day of a party—perhaps a dinner for close friends or an open house to celebrate spring—Clint organizes the meal while Susan rounds up serving pieces, arranges flowers, and sets the table. Throughout the day, with classical music in the background, Susan moves at an even pace. She takes a break to admire an armful of just-cut lilacs from the yard. Clint needs an opinion about the sauce he's just finished. Working together allows time for tennis or a walk on the beach before their guests arrive. When everyone raves about the trouble Susan and Clint have gone to, these hosts can honestly say, "It was no trouble at all."

CoCo, more lap dog than guard dog, waits for guests.

S usan's designer's eye couldn't resist the wit and whimsy of this iced-tea set crafted by American glass artisans. Ordinary iced tea becomes a great deal more worldly when prepared according to Clint's secret formula, which includes tea, orange juice, and spices garnished with mint (recipe, p. 259).

A bowed window in the living room is the perfect spot for an assortment of food, set out on the cherished Dutch-style trunk, overpainted with an Oriental motif, that once belonged to Susan's grandmother. Some guests find a comfortable chair and dine lap style; some prefer a proper place at the table on the porch; others picnic on the lawn.

On the trunk, a delicate arrangement of lilies and willow branches in a twig vase draws the eye upward. Serving food from different heights provides more surface space: a pedestal-style serving bowl and a small footstool handpainted by the artist Charles Muise achieve this end. Mock Foie Gras (recipe, p. 259) occupies the important center position; Champagne bubbles in streamlined flutes with colored stems.

A shallow basket set on the ottoman has been lined with evergreens, an appropriate bed for the western-style serving plate. The wild horse appears to have met his match in a tidal wave of Marinated Cherry Tomatoes (recipe, p. 260).

A thoroughly original find was the copper shopping bag by the Vermont tinsmith Eric Kirchner, which comes in handy for long baguettes. A splash of fancy vinegar from an equally fancy bottle adds dash to the meal.

ALL THE BEST INTENTIONS

Late-summer flowers arranged in a Shaker bucket welcome guests to the front deck of our beach house on Long Island. The happy combination includes Queen Anne's lace, bright yellow coreopsis, and purple verbena. Chester, the sweet stray we adopted from a local animal shelter, appears to appreciate my arrangement.

My own entertaining is undertaken with the best intentions—of doing it all. My cookbook collection—assembled a decade ago when I was a publishing executive at a company that excelled in fine cookbooks—is far more extensive and ambitious than my own abilities. Cookbooks are bedtime reading for me, and hundreds of carefully considered notations on yellow stickers represent big plans for the future. So I begin by looking over the selections and soon become overwhelmed by the enormousness of the meal I have planned. I somehow wisely return to the recipes I know, the seasonal foods that my guests always enjoy. Because it's often more fun to improvise as I go along, I'll begin with a basic main dish—a roasted chicken, for example—and then add whatever our country garden or the local market has in abundance that day. A bowl of fresh peaches always draws more compliments than a tricky soufflé that *almost* rose above the rim.

Our frequent guest, the decorative painter Charles Muise, gave this old French watering can a second life just for me. I use it for flowers —just-cut cosmos resting under shady pines — more often than for its intended function.

I have a friend whose home is "done" each week by a florist. The arrangements are lovely, but I can't imagine being deprived of the joy of working with flowers myself, finding wonderful and surprising combinations, and getting most of the names right. Rather than pillaging our small flower garden in the country, I'll supplement my arrangements with flowers from a farm garden nearby. The woman who owns the farm lets me wander through her fields with one of the children who helps out during the season. Together, we chat about school and summer and flowers, and clip from the endless rows of color. It's nearly impossible to fail when you are merely rearranging nature, since flowers are beautiful and forgiving. I wouldn't think of letting a florist rob me of this therapy!

My entertaining goals are these: to make my home look pretty and inviting early in the day, and then forget it; to appreciate at leisure the palette of food that fills my kitchen, a magnificent Pavarotti inspiring me to great heights; and to have enough time left to take a bubble bath before my guests arrive. I have learned from experience that it's difficult to make it all mesh! Consequently, I will happily seize the opportunity when a willing guest offers, "Is there anything I can do to help?" "Yes!" I reply, and I hand him a tray to pass or napkins to fold. Those guests are good company, and will be invited again and again.

My husband, Joel, would rather harvest his garden for me than share in the meal preparations. Occasionally, he'll be pressed into doing his famous Caesar salad, but his forte is service and clean-up. A former Navy supply officer, he springs to action with military efficiency at just the right times, collecting buffet plates and clanking away in the kitchen.

Our favorite parties—city or country style—are the spontaneous ones, when friends just somehow manage to gather on the spur of the moment. New Yorkers never have enough space, so we are forced into being creative. There's a long tall cupboard in the pantry where I can quickly put my hands on three generations of family china, my etched glassware collection that mixes and

All four vessels on the display surface of our open shelving are by the same anonymous artisan, identified only by a potter's mark—a horseshoe-shaped E. I bought them for very little in Greenwich Village in the early seventies. The small drawing is by Daniel Hale. The sculptural candle holders were handcrafted by Gary Magakis. Sometimes this effective grouping becomes my centerpiece.

Simplicity is the key to enjoying a second home. The English-style oak table, our very first furniture purchase some twenty-five years ago, is large enough to seat eight comfortably, and spacious enough for large buffets.

I

t's a shame to put the things you love in dark cupboards where they're rarely seen. So we keep our tabletop accessories displayed on open shelves. Since everything's within easy reach, I can set a pretty table in record time. When we entertain buffet style, the newly made French iron plate rack doubles as a service area for the Claudia Reese dinnerware, each handcrafted piece of a different design. The ruby-accented champagne glasses, which I also use for wine or juice, are hand blown in Scotland.

matches dozens of designs, and all the unique handcrafted serving pieces by American artisans that I sold at Sweet Nellie, the Madison Avenue shop I owned for eight years. I keep the assorted tabletop accessories—the vases, candle holders, baskets, and candles (I am particular about want-ing hand-dipped candles only; the colors and surfaces are so much lovelier)—in a deep closet off the entrance hall. My antique linens are folded neatly in a wide chest of drawers; the new things are kept in pull-out shelves that have been custom built into a kitchen counter. So I really don't have to think twice when company comes unex-pectedly; everything is there and ready.

With the popularity of take-out salads, microwaveable gourmet foods, and sauces invented by movie stars, I often lament that my best culinary efforts have gone largely unnoticed by our teenage daughter, Erica. I de-cided long ago that I had failed miserably at passing along an appreciation of tasteful manners and, well, the value of Mom's apple pie.

Just as I had given up hope, I returned home late one Saturday to find Erica and seven of her classmates seated around our dining room table having dinner. This time, there were no ravaged empty boxes of pizza littering the tablescape. Instead, candlelight washed over a table set for royalty, right down to my treasured eighteenth-century Hawkes glasses. The eight girls had spent the afternoon shopping for dinner, making tomato sauce from scratch, and finding effervescent cider for their toasts. With Bach for background music, the mood was almost reverential. I soon learned that the event was a celebration of college acceptances and approaching graduation. In my heart, I was celebrating a great deal more. Without much ado—and not one word of caution about clinking the glasses too zealously during the toasts—I left the room, feeling amply rewarded.

Entertaining is a joy for me when I can keep it informal and avoid getting bogged down in the workaday details that frequently leave the host in dire need of an aspirin and a nap. That's why I take advantage of other cooks' talents by occasionally ordering out for more complicated dishes. The Barefoot Contessa in nearby East Hampton has done a beautiful job on their Barefoot Contessa Turkey Breast with Spinach Stuffing and Ina's Bread Pudding (recipes, p. 260). I prepare our own fresh garden Cucumbers with Yogurt-and-Dill Dressing, whip up simple Ginger Beets (recipes, p. 261), and slice luscious tomatoes minutes before serving. The Wild Rice Salad with Avocado and Tahini Dressing (recipe, p. 261) can be made well in advance. Our mothers would not have dreamed of allowing the work of another cook at their tables; today's smart and busy host knows there is plenty of praise to go around.

Looking more like a snowy day than bread pudding, dessert is dressed up with the leaves and blossoms of a strawberry plant and a few fat blackberries.

Even the late-summer garden is a treasure trove of edible flowers, in this case a giant marigold.

 e some-
times forget that our food
and our serving dishes look
all the more appealing
when they are dressed up
with pretty garnishes.
Here, a few snips of thyme
and a nosegay of chive
blossoms are settled in
among lemon leaves near
the turkey breast.

Dill blossoms are a fitting garnish for a dill-seasoned salad, set off in a bowl handcrafted by Judy Kogod.

My weakness for pottery means that an army of wonderful handcrafted serving pieces must each wait their turn to be shown off. The country scene that Donna McGee has painted on her shallow bowl is like a small window waiting for discovery. I use Daniel Mack's twig-handled barbecue pieces for serving.

The work of the potters McKenzie-Childs appeals to me because of its whimsical interpretation of traditional styles. Unusual earthenware pottery adapts well to both formal and informal tables.

An over-sized wide-rimmed plate like this brightly glazed piece by Julie Cline can serve everything from entrees to desserts.

Used for sushi, hors d'oeuvres, or asparagus, this long scalloped dish by Fioriware adds drama and an interesting shape to a buffet arrangement.

Dinner for two is still en- | setting sun, which no other
tertaining. Joel and I often | room in the house offers.
move an old country bench | We've set the bench for din-
from the hallway into the | ner by turning napkins di-
porch room so that we can | agonally and using them
enjoy a view of the | as place mats.

onight's fresh catch is Grilled Swordfish Steaks with Red Pepper Sauce (recipe, p. 261) served with Sesame Green Beans (recipe, p. 262) and New Potatoes with Rosemary (recipe, p. 263). The peppery taste of nasturtiums in salads has made me a convert to edible flowers. The rose-motif plates were designed for Sweet Nellie Designs by Kate Williams, and summer foods look especially appealing on them. A single votive candle ringed with a tendril of garden ivy is just right for the bench.

We often have herbal tea after dinner, this time accompanying slices of honeydew melon that, by happy coincidence, perfectly match the pale yellow mums. The tea cozy, made of vintage fabric, keeps the tea piping hot long after dessert is finished.

The cookie artist Vivian Adams says that her delicately decorated cookies are more easily made than they may appear at first glance (see recipe, p. 262). I may try making them now that I've completed work on my book!

Regionally

Inspired

The deck of Thom McDavitt's log house, appropriately named Tree Tops, is built on a slope that drops off abruptly into woodland and dense thickets. There are three types of pine trees on this New York property, surrounding the log house that would be more conven-

Thom McDavitt stepped into the role of amateur architect when he purchased a ski-house "kit" and changed its style to something distinctly western. Thom shows off his love for symmetry at the garden entrance, with twin pines, a trellis of wisteria, and decorative pots of evergreens on the deck. The moose antlers mounted under the roof's peak were a gift from a guest.

tionally situated in Wyoming, Colorado, or the wilds of Minnesota. Traditional log "camps" farther upstate in the Adirondacks were actually the inspiration for Thom's choice of design. He liked the rustic quality and the outdoor lifestyle they suggested. The rough-hewn spirit of the lodgepole pine walls and the informal setting allow

A florist during the day and an actor by moonlight, Thom takes advantage of his combined talents to stage a "look" on the deck of Tree Tops. It is tempting to draw a connection between the host's many years playing Curly in Oklahoma! *and the many western-style accessories in his home.*

for casual entertaining—and a home for Thom's four rambunctious Irish setters, a mother and her three offspring.

Thom is a former actor whose favorite roles have been in the musical *Oklahoma!* It is tempting for visitors to draw conclusions about the influence of the fictional West on his real life. Now a florist by day, Thom moonlights in local theater productions, playing roles from Padre in *Man of La Mancha* to Dr. Faustus in *Faust*. Thom claims that his free time at home with friends is "down-to-earth, with only a few theatrical touches saved for my cooking." Thom recalls that his most difficult role was an early real-life job on Wall Street at a stock exchange. Ac-

knowledging his unhappiness but needing the job, Thom adjusted by treating it like just another role. "I play-acted," he says. "With the *Wall Street Journal* under my arm and wearing a conservative three-piece suit, I became a financial fashion statement." When the timing was right, Thom left Wall Street for the theater, and, finally, life at Tree Tops.

Most people go through countless bags of charcoal during the summer months, then forget about their grill for the rest of the year. Thom McDavitt's grill is never put away, even in the winter; he uses it year round. Located on the deck just outside the kitchen door, it stands ready for Thom to heat up the coals and toss on marinated chicken, a mix of sausages, several steaks, or fresh fish wrapped in foil. Vegetables go on the grill, too, along with baking potatoes and bread to warm just before serving. "People love the idea of grilling when there's snow on the ground," Thom says. One has sudden flashes of grilling with Dr. Zhivago. . . .

Thom enjoys small impromptu dinners when everyone brings a dish. "It takes the pressure off," he says, "and it's so nice when an enormous salad just arrives." From his growing-up years in New Jersey, Thom recalls community covered-dish suppers, a tradition that is having a renaissance. With his guests numbering anywhere from eight to eighty, Thom says he is grateful for all the help he can get. While one group sets out the food, another is likely to gather round the piano, an old upright with sheet music of show tunes lying open—for a crowd eager to vocalize.

It would not be unusual for guests to go waltzing out onto the deck while four mystified dogs observe the antics of their crazy human friends.

His guests always ask Thom how he gets his clay pots to look so wonderfully grimy! Thom's formula for a naturally aged look is simple: spread buttermilk on the outside of the pots, then place them in a dark, damp area (a basement or under a deck) until moss begins to form. These pots hold spearmint, pineapple mint, and basil. Plant saucers make handy coasters indoors and outdoors.

"It's probably my Irish ancestry," comments Thom wryly about the many plaid tablecloths and napkins he owns. Breakfast in the great outdoors is healthy and trouble free: cottage cheese with fruit, boiled eggs, yogurt with granola, a basket of hot muffins, and another basket of herb bread. Thom likes his apple-patterned pottery because it works both for casual and "formal country" entertaining.

A tacked, leather-sided tray detaches easily from this antique English bar. Set up near the kitchen, it holds ingredients for Bloody Marys. The unusual and rustic log pitcher and mugs are made of cork over ceramic. "Guests get a kick out of asking for a logful," says Thom. A newly crafted toy Adirondack rocker holds softly textured linen napkins.

W hen the weather's nice, dining has indoor-outdoor possibilities with the double doors swung open. The rambling centerpiece—a bed of moss, small pots of variegated ivy, and a pair of antler candlesticks—is suitable for the narrow pine table. An Indian Lake end table handcrafted by the Adirondack furniture maker Ken Heitz has been pulled up to the table for extra serving room. The library-style chandelier, a reproduction of an English antique, pulls down to table height and swivels.

Although Thom has never
visited the Hyde Park Ho-
tel, he likes its vintage restaurant china for the
nostalgia value as well as
for rugged durability. This
tabletop has become a tab-
leau of souvenirs and memories. Charming "cabin"
blocks — reproductions of
antique toys — and wooden
pine trees are Christmas-
tree decorations used out of
season with great success.
The salt and pepper
containers — all gifts from
house guests — have outdoor
themes: a walnut, a log,
and a bear. Even the potatoes seasoned with rose-
mary look rustic.

Dinner is Grilled Mixed Sausages with Sweet Peppers (recipe, p. 262). The vegetables are cooked but still crisp and crunchy. The impressive carving set is crafted from sterling silver and horn.

*T*here's no combination more extravagant than brandy and chocolate. The Center-Stage Chocolate Cake (recipe, p. 263), festooned with roses, tempts even the most reluctant guest. Brandy is served in fine Waterford snifters. Pine branches look natural in a woodland-embossed majolica pitcher.

Antique hooked chair pads
make decorative place mats
for a table even when it's
not being used for dining.
Garden flowers fill an antique cart, probably a toy.

Caiti gets her lounge chair
back when weekend guests
have departed.

THEIR OWN SANTA FE

Guests immediately sense the southwestern mood of this welcoming and tastefully decorated house. Perhaps it's the bright Native American textiles, the many handcrafted baskets and vessels, or the trellised garden, which shows off its colors like a desert sunset. There are touches of the Mediterranean, too, and other sun-drenched countries that remind the home owners—one a writer, the other a financier—of warmth,

Signs and symbols of the Southwest belie the eastern location of this modern home. The terra-cotta vessel is one of many carefully selected decorative objects placed throughout the home and garden.

hospitality, relaxation, and trips they have taken together over the years. The surprise is that a house so convincingly evocative of these regions is located far from its inspirations, in an East Coast community known better for its farmland and ocean views.

The garden has the feeling of an outdoor room, with latticework "walls" surrounding the house for privacy and a trellised pergola overhead for shade. The wire fencing was intended to keep rabbits out, but it further enhances the rustic charm. Substantial wooden garden furniture has weathered nicely with the seasons.

Each room invites visitors to stay a while and explore. The hostess, who enjoys filling up bare walls and empty spaces, has taken great care to fill this airy modern home with treasures ("gifts to the house" is her way of putting it) that she collects or receives as gifts from friends who show they know their hosts' taste. Guests are rewarded in kind. "We want our friends to feel as though they are guests at their own private resort," says the hostess, who fills the comfortable guest room with flowers, leaves a bottle of spring water and the latest novel on the night table, and pampers her guests with soft towels and pretty

bed linens. This couple remembers the old-fashioned courtesies involved in entertaining, and they lavish attention on their guests. "I can't relax until every detail is right," says the high-energy hostess. "We do a lot of running around," she cheerfully admits, but there is pleasure for the couple in providing the many small gestures and nuances that make a difference.

They prefer time with their two teenage children—a son and a daughter—and with their friends over time in the kitchen. "I buy well, but I don't do a lot of complicated cooking" is the hostess's candid comment. "I don't enjoy going into the kitchen at eleven A.M. and doing all that endless chopping! But, on the other hand, I could spend hours arranging the flowers and setting a beautiful table," she adds. The secret to their delicious meals with a minimum of bother is fresh food cooked simply and topped off with store-bought pies and cakes. Lunch around the pool might be cold chicken, pasta with pesto, and a tossed salad. They're likely to prepare an entire dinner for a small group on the grill: fresh fish brushed with lemon butter, local corn, marinated vegetables on skewers, potatoes wrapped in foil, and a loaf of French bread warming on the side. "You can barbecue hot dogs if the evening's exciting and filled with good company," says the hostess.

A close friend and frequent guest—frustrated at not being able to find just the right house gift—knew her search was over when she spotted this decorative gourd being sold by the artisan on a San Francisco street. She filled the dried gourd with pistachio nuts and presented this thoughtful gift to her hosts, who were touched by the gift and the effort.

A cheerful color scheme adds warmth to light, airy rooms. Travel memories of the Mediterranean and a love of western history helped this couple decide on south-western decor, spiced with influences from the many foreign countries they've visited over the years.

The living room is a veritable feast for the eye. Richly textured throws from Guatemala and squares of soft cowhide have been made into comfortable sofa pillows. The Kasoda stone table provides a generous surface for the display of everything from a signed Jimbo Davila folk-art snake to a pair of old spurs.

A baked potato for break-fast is easy and delicious. Here, it is stuffed with grated sharp cheddar cheese and hot chili peppers (see recipe, p. 264, for other stuffing and topping suggestions).

Their liveliest occasions come at times when the house is filled with teenagers—their own and the children of their guests, who are always welcome. "We have our best time when the kids are here," they say. And they might well add, "especially in the summertime." That's when everyone "hangs out" at the pool, plays backgammon, and has long, late dinners. The hostess stocks up on homemade brownies, chocolate-chip cookies, lots of guacamole, chips, and pistachio nuts—a favorite.

The couple's "resort" philosophy works with family and friends, and everyone enjoys the vacation.

The seats of the green-painted bar stools from New Mexico have been covered in cowhide. A vividly painted Guatemalan processional—originally used as a traveling altar in festivals and funerals—now serves as a wall cabinet.

A festive lunch, complete with chilly margaritas and a Southwestern Salad of fresh sliced, diced, and shredded vegetables with a tangy vinaigrette (recipes, p. 263), is awaiting a houseful of guests. Western stone has once again been used as a table surface. Woven mats placed vertically are more practical and graceful on a round table. A table this large can handle a dramatic centerpiece, such as this stunning twig basket with typical Indian markings. The red begonia might not be indigenous to New Mexico, but it certainly looks the part! According to the hosts, their useful lazy Susan makes for some humorous moments when guests get carried away spinning it.

Fascinated by primitive Indian art on canyon walls in Utah, the former Denver steel industry executive Fred Myers gave up a successful career to create imaginative steel sculpture in the style of the originals that inspire him. His dynamic work gives new life to this ancient art. In this home, it is especially fitting, a visual delight for dinner guests.

When this busy couple travels, they take pleasure in using leisure hours to shop and think about "gifts for the house." Recent gifts include small wooden bowls for holding salt and pepper, verdigris reptile candle holders by the craftsman Jonathan Bonner, and a blue wooden charger that can double as a serving platter. The geometric dishes and brushed-metal flatware were ordered from catalogs in another kind of shopping spree.

*If the house is predomi-
nantly southwestern in
mood, then the pool area is
definitely Mediterranean.
Remaining true to their belief that guests should feel
transported to a carefree
resort setting while at their
house, the hosts have created many choices for
lounging and getting away
from it all.*

Frosted and etched, the glassware sits ready before the start of a late-afternoon cocktail party.

Easily movable serving carts that match the garden furniture are handy for large cocktail parties. It goes without saying that the food for this party has a south-of-the-border flavor.

Zesty Melon Salsa (recipe, p. 264) is a sweet and mild variation of its better-known relative. It's great with chips or as a condiment for broiled or grilled fish. Bite-size pieces of lightly sautéed or grilled vegetables on skewers are easy and appealing. Flat carrying baskets with handles are a must.

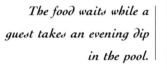

A few fresh leaves and flowers decorate a basket of
meat-filled empanadas.
Sangría and the Southwest
are synonymous.

The food waits while a
guest takes an evening dip
in the pool.

Celebrations

A GENEROSITY OF SPIRIT

On the stairs by the dining room in Dennis Berger's carriage-house home, richly colored kale plants alternate with small perfect pumpkins, a salute to harvest time and a welcome to guests who have been invited to participate and to celebrate at dinner. The brass horn is part of the host's collection of old musical instruments.

To find Dennis Berger's charming 1846 carriage house in New York's Greenwich Village, visitors must first locate the wrought-iron gate without a name or a number, then the rusty intercom. In daylight, this is difficult; at night, visitors are advised to bring a flashlight.

A dark and narrow passageway from the street— the old horse route—leads to Dennis's home. Visitors are somehow unprepared for the secluded courtyard beyond, which is filled with direct sunlight. Street noises suddenly vanish, and the rustle of autumn leaves commands attention.

An advertising creative director who has written

After a dark walk through a narrow passageway, guests are pleasantly surprised to come upon a bright courtyard at the entrance to Berger's home. Pumpkins and potted kale welcome guests by the front door.

many famous and upbeat campaigns, this host lives in the same style as his slogans. Dennis thinks and creates in broad strokes and enjoys entertaining in an ample way. His wine collection is extensive; his oversized furniture is meant for sinking into for the evening.

"I like the meal to be the main attraction," Dennis says, adding that the wine should be a delicious match for the meal but should not upstage it. He hopes his guests will return home with memories of good company and a hearty dinner. "A delicate bed of lettuce with sprouts is not my idea of a good time," he says, looking to rich pasta recipes for the sort of satisfying food he loves. It's difficult for guests to duplicate one of Dennis's recipes, because this host creates dishes by instinct. Adding a pinch of this and a dash of that, Dennis takes full

advantage of whatever is in the refrigerator or the cup-board whenever someone stops by.

Entertaining for a group of friends is usually a com-munal effort. His kitchen is part of the main downstairs room of the former carriage house. Bringing wine would be redundant. So invited guests bring fresh offerings from markets and bakeries—Bosc pears, dinner rolls, pretty kale plants—and help with the tabletop decor. Dennis assumes the major responsibility in the kitchen, but rarely begins any preparation ahead of time. "Since my meals are large, I like my desserts to be light—fruit, sorbets, fruit pies." He advises against scrimping on fine ingre-dients; otherwise the effort may be a disappointment.

This popular bon vivant has very definite ideas about entertaining. The carriage house has windows on only one side, so candlelight is common even when the sun is shining. He prefers small informal gatherings of four to six, and the charm and intimacy of his home are perfectly compatible with this preference. He recalls his most memorable dinner party: "It was a small party outdoors in the courtyard for six, featuring beautiful Dunge-ness crabs and equally wonderful light rain showers—just as we sat down to eat."

Dennis readily admits to sometimes living larger than life. His interests are varied, and are reflected in his possessions: a wall of fine vintage wines; a collection of antique clocks and clock signs, looming large like some Dalí dreamscape; a collection of Bakelite radios, which Dennis enjoys now and remembers fondly from his child-hood; massive architectural remnants; and an old sign from a town in Wisconsin that bears his first name. The good-natured enthusiasm Dennis Berger has for his friends is echoed in a famous slogan he created: "We bring good things to life." And he does indeed.

D*ennis enjoys entertaining in an ample way. His wine collection — red only — is extensive, his glasses hold double the usual amount, and his oversized furniture is meant for sinking into.*

A reproduction game board by the artisan Robin Lankford doubles as a tray, holding the just-poured wine. Small clay pots filled with smooth black stones hold candles. An artist friend has turned Brussels-sprouts topiaries into sculpture by enclosing them in gold-painted chicken wire, an unexpected coffee-table decoration.

Dennis Berger had some reservations when an artist friend arrived with a roll of chicken wire in one hand and a can of gold spray paint in the other. But Dennis gave her free rein with a few unorthodox ideas, such as a gilded wire table runner, a testimony to his own creativity and faith in his friend's ability to pull off the project with panache. Fall leaves have been sprayed lightly with gold, allowing the leaves' own golden-brown color to show through.

Fall offerings —
branches of bittersweet,
crab apples, and leaves
gathered in the country —
cascade down the table in
imitation of Nature's au-
tumn landscape. The leaves
and the gilded wire reflect
the candlelight.

"I like my meals to be abundant—more than anyone can eat," Dennis says. A course of hearty Pumpkin Peanut Soup (recipe, p. 264) certainly attests to that. Even the fully rounded bowls of the sterling soup spoons speak of hearty portions! The individual bowls and the large pumpkin soup tureen were designed by the ceramicist Barbara Eigen. The acorn squash bowls have been placed on square slab-glass plates created by artisans at Annieglass.

A friend has brought yeast rolls baked in lead-free terra-cotta flowerpots, a clever presentation for breads.

Guests

A wall of wine, which takes on a second life as conceptual art, advertises the host's passion for fine and rare wines. A handmade guest book is filled with warm and lavish words of thanks from Berger's guests.

One dictionary defines a pumpkin as "a large orange fruit on a vine." Who knows where the great pumpkin is lurking. . . .

This 1868 Victorian farmhouse is graced with the history of the landed gentry who lived there and gave it its simple and appropriate name: Daybreak. Facing east, the house catches the first rays of daylight. Slated for possible eminent-domain repossession many years ago, the property was bought by a young mother and real estate broker—Mona Schmidt—who took a chance that the highway proposed for the location would not be built.

Built in 1868, Daybreak is blessed with exquisite detailing, which has been much admired by guests and appreciated by four generations of family.

She bought the house and waited. Today, the Long Island countryside remains as it was then; the rolling lawns and woodlands of Daybreak are now the playground for Mona's grandchildren and a place where four generations can gather.

A wreath of pomegranates, pinecones, boxwood, and juniper was created especially for Daybreak and its owners, Mona and Larry O'Rourke, by the floral artist Carol Pflumm. The tips of the pinecones have been snipped off so each one resembles a flower. Small artichokes painted gold catch the sunlight.

Daybreak has enjoyed a happy abundance of family celebrations. Mona held a wedding reception for one of her daughters here, in the garden and under a tent on the terrace. With the organization of a professional wedding coordinator, she handled every last detail and managed to arrange all the flowers, too. Then, several years ago, her own marriage to Lawrence O'Rourke took place in the same garden, when all the hydrangeas were in bloom.

Celebrations at the house, especially Christmas, honor Swedish family traditions. Everyone wants the glögg that is heating on the big stove in the kitchen. "It's an outrageous concoction of liquors and spices that warms you quickly and prepares you for the family smorgasbord," Mona warns. This traditional punch recipe was passed down to Mona by her Swedish mother, who now has two granddaughters and two great-grandchildren to carry on the recipe and the tradition.

There is never a shortage of glasses or dinnerware for family occasions or for grand-scale parties. Mona quickly admits to being an early bird when it comes to tag sales and flea markets. Freely admitting to this one addiction, Mona reveals ceiling-high cupboards and vaultlike closets filled with carefully arranged possessions, each a distinctive acquisition purchased at an amazing price. A single candle holder missing its match is treasured as much as a complete set of etched wineglasses. In fact, Mona and Larry have a collection of candle holders that numbers thirty and counting. At Christmas, she sometimes decks all five mantels with candles and uses only candlelight for a dinner at dusk.

A trip to the attic is an experience. Mona has stored the makings of a traditional Christmas in an untold number of cardboard boxes, each containing enough ornaments and pinecones to decorate several homes. The pine cones are grouped according to size—small, medium, and large. The trolls come in sizes too. There are lights for trees inside and out, and garlands of tinsel for every tree and more. At holiday time, it becomes necessary to edit down the Christmas decorations to a manageable number. Perhaps there is something in Mona's Swedish blood that accounts for the joy with which she celebrates Christmas.

Throughout Christmas Day, the old floorboards creak with the weight of skipping children and newly arrived guests, who head for the glögg. The scent of recently gathered pinecones and greens fills the air and refreshes weary travelers. At Daybreak, *skol* is a Swedish greeting with a distinctly American accent.

Mona O'Rourke, whose family roots are Scandinavian, begins her Christmas plans long before the first cold snap. She was amused to see the same satin dress fabric that she bought at a discount outlet in October on a department store mannequin in December, carrying a designer label. Here, she's created a dramatic swag for the simple pine mirror in the entrance hall. A garland hugs the banister, intertwined with gold ribbon.

A Heisey glass vase (left) and a contemporary piece of glassware hold a glittering combination of new decorations and heirloom tree ornaments given to Mona by her mother.

The stove is a 1929 Magic Chef, upon which a brew of Swedish Glögg (recipe, p. 264) awaits family and friends. Pine boughs and cones from the yard are nestled in a basket above the stove, spreading the scent of a wintry day.

An antiquarian book with a handsome binding is a thoughtful holiday gift, especially when it's wrapped in gold ribbon and presented with a bunch of fragrant cinnamon sticks.

Everyone has been waiting for the glögg! Ladled hot from the stove, it is served in glass cups on a heart-shaped copper tray.

Preserved Eggplant (recipe, p. 265), presented in old mason jars and decorated with an old-fashioned

A handcrafted gift, such as this one-of-a-kind painted box by the artist Charles Muise, is made all the sweeter when it's filled with home-baked Chocolate Nut Cookies (recipe, p. 265).

label, looks as though it came from Grandmother's pantry. It's easy to make and great to give as a gift.

Amy
Your Favorite!
Love ~
Mother

Vintage fabric cut with pinking shears makes a sweet cap for this jar of whole almonds in pure natural honey, delicious when spooned over ice cream or vanilla yogurt.

P retty etched-glass bottles from a housewares catalog have been filled first with garlic and fresh herbs — thyme, tarragon, and basil — then with a good cider vinegar (recipe, p. 265). Small bundles of dried herbs or flowers may be tied on with decorative bows. The longer the vinegar sits, the better it tastes.

With five fireplaces and, therefore, five mantels in the house, Mona decorates all of them with holiday greens, lights, ornaments, and other decorative trim, beginning here in the spacious living room.

With an eye for variations in texture and contrast, some of the elements for the living room mantel arrangement were selected from a local garden center and include juniper branches and dried hy-drangea. Pinecones, ranging in size from tiny to gigantic, come from the yard. Dried roses from past bouquets add color; rhododendron leaves spray-painted in gold add a festive note.

Boxwood and pepper berries have been pushed into the Styrofoam "trunk" of this table tree, the base of which is covered with moss. Dried hydrangeas spiral around it, creating a softly romantic effect. The corner cupboard, Mona's pride and joy, holds her "mish-mash" of china, crystal, and silver, including English blueware, French porcelain, and leaded glass — whole collections as well as wonderful single and unmatched discoveries.

Following pages: luminescent mussel shells, souvenirs from a walk on the beach, add interest to an unexpected arrangement on a painted glass coffee table in the living room. The table surface reflects light from the candles in small pressed-glass holders.

Late-afternoon sun dances over the table in the O'Rourke dining room. Mona was especially happy to receive the tobacco-leaf-pattern plates as a wedding gift when she and Larry married; she has owned napkins with that same pattern for some twenty-five years. The blue glasses are from a garage sale. By odd coincidence, Larry owned a set of the exact same glasses, from an inheritance.

It's an effort to carry the cast-iron birdbath—one of Mona and Larry's favorite wedding gifts—from the garden to the dining room, but it's worth it. Cupid sits smugly in the center of the table, his lap filled with fruit and gold-dusted seasonal greens.

Mona can't pass up the vintage linens and countless tabletop collectibles she finds at flea markets and antiques shops in the area. A small napkin bouquet is lovingly made for each guest from extra greens and dried flowers. The cotton moiré tablecloth works as a subtle backdrop for the stronger colors of the china and glassware.

*S*mall bird lights
are nestled in a mantel
arrangement over the
dining-room fireplace,
where greens, dried leaves,
branches from a money
plant, and seasonal fruits
work effectively together.

The outdoors is again brought indoors, this time with a verdigris garden urn, one of a pair placed on the Hepplewhite sideboard, next to antique crystal candle holders. The fruit is kept from tumbling by strategically placed toothpicks.

A FAMILY FOURTH

Sand won't spoil the annual Kennedy-Kirkwood Fourth of July clambake on the beach. Colorful gift boxes filled with all the essential picnic accessories serve as useful lap trays.

During the early part of the century, the seven-hundred-acre Bell estate was one of the most impressive waterfront enclaves on the far-eastern end of Long Island. One can only imagine the elegant parties and balls that took place at the mansion at the height of the Belle Epoque. The house's unobstructed cliffside view across Gardiner's Bay to the Atlantic was as spectacular then as it is now. In addition to the grand house, Dr. Bell constructed seven related outbuildings on the property, including a gate house to keep away intruders and a carriage house for the horse-drawn fleet. In recent times, the property has been tastefully developed into individual home sites with thoughtful attention to its historical integrity.

An American flag—showing signs of wear from well meaning patriotism over the years—has been draped over the railing at the end of the walkway to the bay beach where the clambake is held.

James and Kristine Kennedy had just married when they decided that the gate house, a modest yet charming structure, could be their dream house—with a little vision and a lot of scraping and stripping. They called their new home Broad Gate. It helped that Jim and Kristine had good neighbors—Kristine's large family, who was renovating the old carriage house just a short walk away. When their first child, James, was born, he had built-in baby-sitters clamoring to take turns.

The yard surrounding Jim and Kristine Kennedy's 1910 gate house, which they call Broad Gate, was overgrown when they bought the property. Mistaken for a hunter by flying scavengers, this scarecrow now keeps order there every summer.

The Kennedys' property was rich with grapevines that simply needed pruning and staking. A pinwheel keeps the crows at bay.

A new generation at the Bell estate has given rise to a new kind of family occasion, especially during the summer months. A long stretch of sandy bay beach is a mere eighty-four steps down the cliff, as measured by the original funicular, which is still in use. Summer means picnics and bonfires, with the best of everything saved for the family Fourth of July celebration. When the Fourth arrives, everyone springs into action and heads in different directions: to the fish market for the seafood, to the farm stand for the tomatoes and the corn; to the beach to dig the clam pit; then back and forth with the Jeep to haul the food and the gear. At Broad Gate, young James and his grandmother pack up red gift boxes that will serve as clever and festive lap trays and contain everything guests need to enjoy a clambake—from patriotic paper plates to prepackaged hand wipes. James's mother puts the final touches on her famous salad of local tomatoes and blue cheese, which she carefully carries to the beach in the largest bowl she owns.

As the sun begins to disappear behind the cliff and the bay breezes pick up, the clan and good friends gather on the beach. The spot never changes, so there's no need to give directions. Soon the lobsters on the grill are bright red, and the corn husks are pleasingly charcoaled all over. A tub of ice keeps the beer and Long Island wine chilly while a captive audience awaits the annual fireworks display. As tradition dictates, everyone stays till long after the last burst of fireworks has fallen into the bay.

A leisurely breakfast in the living room — the main attraction being Bountiful Board French Toast (recipe, p. 265) — is a sure sign it's the weekend. Delicate botanical china looks especially pleasing with soft-yellow napkins that are also used as place mats. A ceramic berry carrier filled with blackberries is also perfect for serving crudités and dip.

A formal room, showing off Kristine's love for English things, the Kennedys' gracious living room is not reserved for company only, but frequently enjoyed by Jim, Kristine, and their four-year-old son, James, who can sit in his very own antique deck chair, recently refinished by his mother.

T he backs of open cupboards are wallpapered to match the walls, creating a sense of extended space in the diminutive kitchen. Irish crystal, among the couple's treasured wedding gifts, fills the shelves. A contented kitchen cow decorates the backsplash.

The whole family gets into the act for the clambake, and the cooking and packing begin at Broad Gate. Exotic Gazpacho (recipe, p. 266), packed in mason jars decorated with patriotic bands, has been prepared extra thick with home-grown tomatoes. It will thin in consistency as the ice melts on the ride to the beach. Everyone drinks the chilled soup from forties-style plastic glasses while they wait for the fish and vegetables to cook.

Each picnic box has been lined with a lace doily. Then into the box go foil-coated paper plates, whimsical claw-shaped crackers, and plastic utensils tucked in pockets of star-spangled cotton napkins. The small American flags were found in an abandoned box on the carriage-house property; the forty-eight stars would date them at sometime before 1959.

A clambake for a crowd is a big undertaking, so the whole family divides the tasks. Grandpa loads the Jeep with James's uncle John and aunt Jaclene, who also dig the pit and put up the coals.

The location of the clambake is traditional: at the end of a long boardwalk that family and guests will use to get to the beach.

N ewly distressed reproductions of old lobster carriers are just the thing to tote the makings of a clambake: live lobsters, local corn, and clams and mussels in net bags.

Two large grates have been placed side by side over the hot pit. New potatoes cook in heavy frying pans with olive oil, a pat of butter, and a good sprinkling of sea salt. The corn, stripped of its topmost tuft of silk, is grilled in the husk just above the coals.

The shellfish rests on a bed of seaweed so that it is steamed by the hot coals. The result is a feast with a wonderful briny flavor. *This is a simplified variation of a traditional clambake, and it involves many willing hands (recipe, p. 266).*

Plastic wineglasses provide a touch of elegance on the beach, chilling in an old copper kettle along with the cold drinks.

The daily special at the fish market was New Zealand kiwi mussels, with luminescent greenish shells.

Along with the location and the guest list, many of the foods have become annual traditions. "Everyone just expects my salad," says Kristine of her Cherry Tomato and Blue Cheese Salad (recipe, p. 266), "and I wouldn't think of disappointing this crowd!"

The feast is set out on a makeshift groaning board constructed from lobster pots laid end to end.

Citronella torches help keep bugs away for guests who stay for the fireworks. Paper bags with decorative cutouts have been filled with sand, which secures votive candles in the bottom of the bags and anchors them against evening breezes.

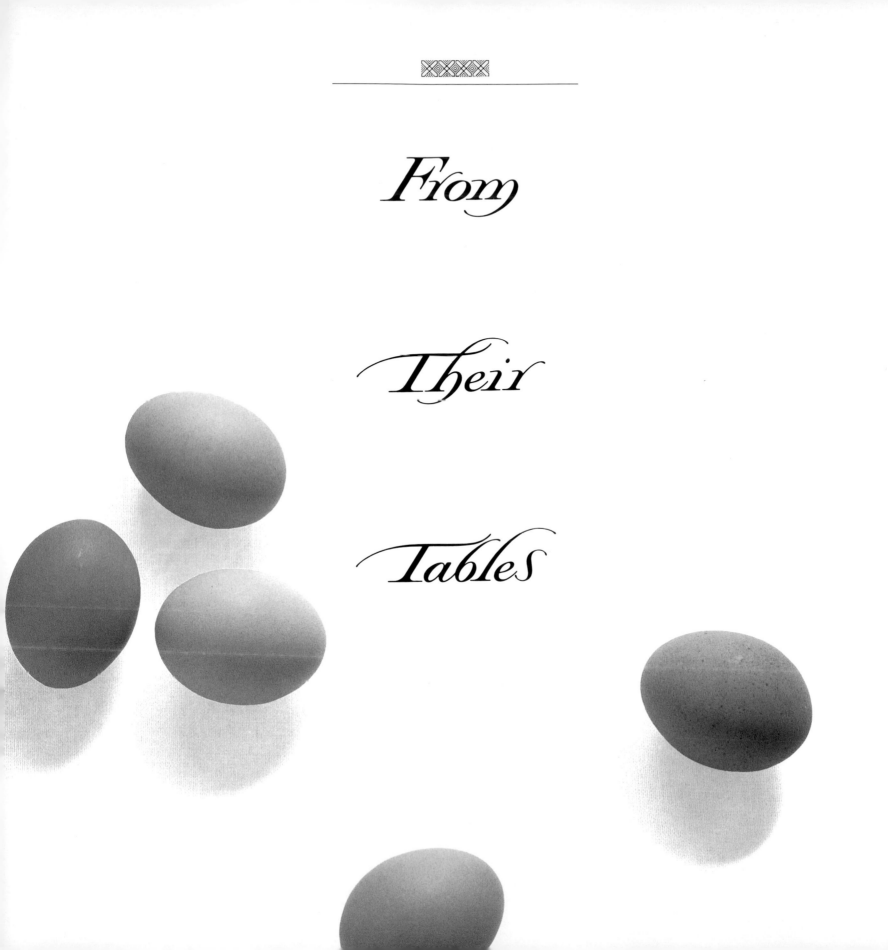

From

Their

Tables

THE RECIPES

EGG-AND-SAUSAGE SOUFFLÉ

This complete brunch dish, rich and filling, can be assembled the night before serving.

8 slices white bread, crusts removed

1/4 pound hot sausage patties (or bulk), browned and drained

1/4 pound sweet sausage patties (or bulk), browned and drained

3/4 pound sharp cheddar cheese, grated

4 eggs

3 cups milk

1/2 teaspoon salt

3/4 teaspoon dry mustard

1 10 3/4-ounce can condensed cream of mushroom soup

1 4 1/2-ounce jar mushrooms, coarsely chopped

Cut the bread into 1-inch cubes and layer them in the bottom of a 9 × 13-inch baking dish. Top with cooked sausage and grated cheese. Beat together the eggs, 2 1/2 cups of the milk, salt, and mustard. Pour over casserole, cover, and refrigerate overnight.

The next morning, mix the soup, mushrooms, and remaining milk together and pour over the casserole. Bake in a preheated 300-degree oven for 1 hour, 15 minutes, or until casserole is browned and bubbling.

Serves 4 to 6.

LAZY BANANA BLUEBERRY MUFFINS

This recipe takes advantage of the baking mix that our mothers used to swear by when they were in a hurry. A few frills have been added.

1 egg, beaten

1/2 cup milk

3 cups packaged baking mix

2 very ripe medium-size bananas, mashed (should be about 1 cup)

3/4 cup sugar

3/4 cup chopped walnuts

1 1/2 cups fresh blueberries

Beat egg and milk together. Add remaining ingredients, except berries, and mix well. Fold in blueberries. Spoon mixture into well-greased muffin tins, filling them three-quarters full, and bake in a preheated 350-degree oven 15 to 18 minutes, or until brown. Allow to cool in tins 5 minutes before removing.

Makes 18 large muffins.

PAPAYA SALAD WITH TANGY DRESSING

The papaya and lettuce combination is refreshing, but if papayas are unavailable, substitute oranges.

1/2 cup sugar or honey

1 teaspoon salt

1/2 teaspoon dry mustard

1/2 cup white wine vinegar

1 cup vegetable oil

3 tablespoons chopped onion

2 tablespoons papaya seeds (optional)

2 heads romaine lettuce

2 papayas, peeled, seeded, and sliced into wedges

1 red onion, sliced and separated into rings

Combine the first seven ingredients in a food processor and puree until smooth. (This dressing will keep for up to three days in the refrigerator.) Wash the lettuce leaves, pat dry, and tear into bite-size pieces. Toss together the lettuce, papaya, onion, and dressing and serve immediately.

Serves 8.

WINTER VEGETABLE CASSEROLE

3 unpeeled baking potatoes, thinly sliced

Salt and pepper to taste

¼ teaspoon freshly grated nutmeg

2 rutabagas, peeled and thinly sliced

1 celery root, trimmed, peeled, and thinly sliced

4 tablespoons (½ stick) cold butter, cut into cubes

1 large onion, sliced

1½ cups heavy cream

¾ cup grated Parmesan cheese

4 tablespoons (½ stick) melted butter

1 cup whole-wheat or sourdough bread crumbs

Layer the potato slices in the bottom of a buttered 9 × 13-inch baking dish. Sprinkle with salt, pepper, and nutmeg. Follow with a layer of rutabagas, then a layer of celery root, and finish with a layer of onions, topping each layer with a sprinkling of the seasonings. Dot the top of the casserole with cubes of cold butter. Pour cream over top, cover tightly with foil, and bake in a preheated 350-degree oven for 1 hour.

Meanwhile, toss together the cheese, melted butter, and bread crumbs. After 1 hour, remove casserole from oven and sprinkle with bread-crumb mixture. Reduce oven temperature to 300. Return casserole, uncovered, to oven and bake for an additional 45 minutes to 1 hour, or until vegetables are tender.

Serves 10 to 12.

AMERICAN CRAB CAKES

Christina Woo at The American Gourmet in Los Angeles originated this spicy recipe. Crabmeat substitute gives the dish a more tender texture and a more assertive flavor, but purists may want to prepare it entirely with real crabmeat.

10 slices good-quality white bread, broken into pieces

1½ teaspoons powdered thyme

½ teaspoon salt

¼ teaspoon cayenne pepper, or more to taste

2 large shallots or ¼ large onion, peeled and cut into pieces

½ pound cooked imitation crabmeat or crabmeat substitute, coarsely flaked

¼ cup Parmesan cheese, grated

1 egg

1 egg yolk

1½ teaspoons mayonnaise

3 teaspoons spicy brown prepared mustard

1½ teaspoons lemon or lime juice

½ pound cooked crabmeat, coarsely flaked

Vegetable oil for frying

DEBORAH'S SAUCE

2 cups mayonnaise

¾ cup chili sauce

2 hard-boiled eggs, chopped

Dash Tabasco sauce

1 tablespoon Worcestershire sauce

Juice of ½ lemon

1 tablespoon capers

In a food processor fitted with a steel blade, combine bread, thyme, salt, and cayenne and process until the mixture turns into fine crumbs.

Transfer contents to a shallow platter or pan and set aside. With the machine running, drop the shallots or onion pieces through the feed tube and chop roughly. Add imitation crabmeat and pulse until fish is finely chopped. Add remaining ingredients, plus half the reserved bread-crumb mixture, and pulse until smooth. Set aside. (The mixture should be moist enough to stick together when formed into patties, but not too wet or the cakes will fall apart in cooking.)

Next, combine all sauce ingredients in a large bowl, cover, and refrigerate. Recipe may be prepared up to this point 1 day ahead; if you do this, cover and refrigerate crab mixture until ready to cook.

The day of serving, shape crab mixture into 10 to 12 patties, dipping each one into the remaining bread-crumb mixture until thoroughly coated on both sides. Heat ⅛ inch of the oil in a skillet or sauté pan. Cook crab cakes over medium-high heat until golden brown on both sides. Drain on several layers of paper towels. Keep cooked cakes warm in the oven while remaining cakes are cooking. Serve hot with Deborah's Sauce on the side.

Serves 6.

CELESTIAL SALAD WITH POMMERY VINAIGRETTE

It's pretty, and it's easy to assemble for a large sit-down affair.

1 tablespoon Pommery mustard
2 tablespoons red wine vinegar
3 tablespoons olive oil, plus more if desired
1 head red-leaf lettuce
2 heads Belgian endive
2 ripe kiwis, peeled and sliced paper thin
1 red onion, peeled and sliced paper thin
3 baby yellow squash, sliced paper thin
Fresh chives

Whisk the first three ingredients together until oil is fully incorporated. For a milder flavor, add an additional tablespoon of oil. Pour into a serving vessel and set aside.

Wash the greens and carefully pat dry. Fan approximately six lettuce leaves on one side of each of four serving plates. Fan six to eight endive leaves on the other side. Layer the kiwi, onion, and squash slices down the center of the plates. Decorate with long slices of fresh chives. Serve with the dressing on the side.

Serves 4.

CHICKEN AND SHRIMP GUMBO

This memorable gumbo for a crowd is worth the extra effort!

6 to 8 cups chicken stock or canned chicken broth
1 3-to-4-pound chicken
1 carrot, 1 peeled onion, and 2 bay leaves for stock
1 tablespoon vegetable oil, or more if necessary
1 pound hot smoked sausage or kielbasa, cut into ½-inch slices
¾ cup flour
1 large red bell pepper, chopped
1 large yellow bell pepper, chopped
1 large onion, peeled and thinly sliced
2 small green chili peppers, seeded and chopped
1 teaspoon dried thyme leaves, crumbled
1 teaspoon filé powder
½ teaspoon dried oregano, crumbled
1 to 2 teaspoons cayenne pepper
1 28-ounce can plum tomatoes (do not drain)
½ pound okra, chopped
1 pound medium-size shrimp, peeled and deveined
Salt and freshly ground pepper to taste
1 cup cooked green peas
3 cups cooked white rice
1 cup chopped scallions

Place the stock in a large stockpot, bring to a boil, then reduce heat to a simmer. Add the chicken, carrot, onion, bay leaves, and enough hot water to cover. Cook until chicken is tender, about 50 minutes. Transfer chicken to a cutting board and strain stock into a large saucepan. Skin and bone the chicken and set chicken meat aside.

Heat the oil in a heavy skillet and sauté the sausage slices over medium heat until brown. Transfer to a platter lined with paper towels and drain. Pour off extra fat from the skillet until ½ cup of fat remains. If less than ½ cup fat remains, add enough oil to make ½ cup.

Add flour to the skillet and blend. Cook over low heat, stirring frequently, for about 45 minutes, or until roux turns a dark caramel-chocolate color. Add the bell peppers, sliced onion, and chili peppers and cook until vegetables are just wilted. Remove from heat and set aside.

Bring the reserved chicken stock back to a boil. Add the roux mixture and blend well. Add spices, browned sausage, and tomatoes with the juice from the can. Simmer for 2 hours, until stock is slightly thickened. Add the cooked chicken meat, shrimp, and okra and cook until shrimp is pink, about 5 to 10 minutes. Add salt and pepper to taste.

Transfer gumbo to a tureen. Combine peas and rice, then spoon about ⅓ cup of this mixture into each of 12 individual serving bowls. Add the gumbo and sprinkle with scallions, sundae style.

Serves 12.

LEMON GLAZE

This lemony sugar glaze is meant to be ladled, hot, over a store-bought bundt-type cake. It could also be used, cooled, on a homemade cake hot from the oven.

1½ cups confectioners' sugar
¼ cup fresh lemon juice
1 tablespoon Grand Marnier, Kirsch, or Cointreau liqueur
2 drops yellow food coloring

Combine sugar and lemon juice in a small saucepan. Bring mixture to a boil, then remove from heat. Stir in liqueur of choice and food coloring. Immediately brush one-half of mixture evenly over top and sides of cake. Then pour the remaining glaze over cake, letting it run down the sides unevenly. Allow the cake to sit for at least an hour before serving.

Makes enough glaze for 1 10-inch cake.

BUTTERMILK CORN STICKS

For a different color, substitute blue cornmeal for the traditional yellow.

1 cup cornmeal
1 cup unbleached flour
2 teaspoons baking powder
½ teaspoon baking soda
½ teaspoon salt
1 egg, beaten
1 cup lowfat buttermilk
⅜ cup honey
3 tablespoons butter, melted and cooled

Preheat oven to 400 degrees. Generously grease two cast-iron cornbread pans and place in oven to heat.

Meanwhile, mix together dry ingredients. Add remaining ingredients and blend well.

Remove pans from oven and fill with batter. Bake at 400 degrees for 15 to 20 minutes, or until slightly golden-brown on top. Serve hot.

Makes 12 sticks.

CONFETTI COLESLAW

Pretty as its name!

1 small head green cabbage, shredded
1 small head red cabbage, shredded
1 medium cucumber, peeled and coarsely chopped
½ red bell pepper, chopped
½ yellow bell pepper, chopped
2 carrots, grated
½ cup mayonnaise
½ cup plain yogurt
2 tablespoons fresh lemon juice
2 tablespoons tarragon vinegar
2 tablespoons honey
1½ teaspoons celery seed
Salt and freshly ground pepper to taste

Toss vegetables together and set aside. Whisk together remaining ingredients until honey is well blended. Pour dressing over vegetables and toss.

Serves 12.

PEACH WALNUT CRISP

This recipe can be adapted to include other seasonal fruits, such as apples and blackberries.

12 peaches, peeled and sliced
2 tablespoons fresh lemon juice
3 tablespoons honey
1 cup unbleached flour
⅓ cup rolled oats (not instant)
1 cup brown sugar, firmly packed
2 teaspoons cinnamon
½ teaspoon freshly grated nutmeg
½ cup (1 stick) cold unsalted butter
½ cup walnuts, coarsely chopped
Vanilla ice cream or whipped cream

Preheat oven to 350 degrees. Butter an 8-inch square cake pan or 9-inch pie plate. Place peaches in pan and drizzle with lemon juice and honey. Toss lightly. In a food processor fitted with a steel blade, blend all remaining ingredients, except the walnuts, until the mixture resembles coarse meal. Sprinkle over peaches, making sure to distribute evenly. Top with nuts. Bake in the preheated oven for about 30 minutes, or until top is lightly browned. Serve warm with whipped cream or vanilla ice cream.

Serves 8.

GRILLED VEGETABLE-CHEESE SANDWICHES

Olive oil
1 zucchini, sliced on the diagonal
1 loaf French bread
Fresh sage leaves
½ pound good melting cheese (such as Gruyère, Comte, mozzarella, or cheddar), sliced to desired thickness
½ red bell pepper, cut in long slices

In a frying pan thinly coated with olive oil, sauté zucchini slices quickly. Drain on paper towels, patting out excess oil. Slice 8 slices of French bread, cutting slightly on the diagonal. Then top each bread slice with two slices of zucchini, then several sage leaves. Top with cheese slices and a sliver of red pepper. Place sandwiches under broiler until cheese melts. Serve immediately.

Serves 4.

Variations: Substitute sautéed eggplant, fresh red pepper, raw onion, or fresh tomato slices for the zucchini. Instead of sage leaves, try fresh basil, oregano, or thyme. Chevre, Swiss, and Muenster are delicious cheese choices.

Place apple slices and raisins on the Fresh bread slices and top with any mild cheese. Place under broiler just to melt cheese. Top with a dollop of horseradish or hot mustard.

FANCY BAKED BRIE

1 large round loaf of hearty white bread, at least 9 inches in diameter
1 8-inch Brie wheel
¼ cup walnut halves
¼ cup dried raisins or cherries
¼ cup slivered almonds
1 to 2 tablespoons dried basil

Carefully hollow out the bread to create a well just large enough to hold the wheel of Brie, reserving the cutout portion of bread. Set the Brie into the hollow and arrange the walnuts on the lower left-hand quadrant of the cheese. On the upper left-hand quadrant, arrange the fruit; on the upper right, the almonds; and on the lower right, the basil. Cut the reserved bread into cubes and set aside.

Bake cheese in a preheated 350-degree oven about 30 minutes, until very soft to the touch and slightly browned. Serve with cubed bread on the side for dipping into the cheese.

Serves 16 to 20 as an hors d'oeuvre.

MINNIE K.'S JELL-O–CARROT SALAD

An uncomplicated dish from a simpler time.

1 3-ounce package lemon-flavored Jell-O
1 8-ounce can crushed pineapple, in its own juice
2 cups grated carrots
1 cup shelled pecans, coarsely chopped

Dissolve Jell-O in 1 cup boiling water. Drain liquid from the pineapple can into a measuring cup and add enough water to make 1 cup of liquid. Stir this liquid into gelatin mixture. Add pineapple, carrots, and pecans. Mix together and pour into a glass baking dish. Refrigerate until firm, about 4 hours.

Serves 6.

SWEET POTATOES WITH MARSHMALLOWS

A tried-and-true southern favorite!

2 16-ounce cans cooked sweet potatoes, drained
Pinch cinnamon
Pinch freshly grated nutmeg
¼ cup freshly squeezed orange juice, or more to taste
½ cup brown sugar, firmly packed, or more to taste
1 10-ounce bag (approximately 53) marshmallows

Mash potatoes in a large bowl. Add cinnamon, nutmeg, brown sugar, and orange juice. Spoon mixture into a 13 × 9-inch baking dish and arrange marshmallows close together on top. Bake in a preheated 350-degree oven for 20 to 30 minutes, or until marshmallows are browned.

Serves 6.

TEMPTING TUNA SALAD

Since this is such a pretty tuna salad, it makes a nice luncheon dish, served on a bed of crisp lettuce.

1 6½-ounce can white albacore tuna, packed in water, drained
1 6½-ounce can chunk light tuna, packed in water, drained
½ cup chopped celery
¼ cup minced onion
¼ cup capers
6 ripe cherry tomatoes, seeded and quartered
1 teaspoon Dijon mustard
1½ tablespoons white wine vinegar
3 tablespoons extra-virgin olive oil
1 to 2 tablespoons dark sesame oil
2 tablespoons honey
Juice of ½ lemon
½ teaspoon ground coriander seeds
½ teaspoon curry powder
1 clove garlic, crushed
Dash of cinnamon
Dash of ground nutmeg

Combine first six ingredients in a mixing bowl. In a separate bowl, combine remaining ingredients, then lightly toss with tuna salad.
Serves 6.

COLD BEET SOUP

Everything goes into a food processor in quick succession for this bright and hearty beet soup, which can also be served hot.

2 large onions, peeled and cut into large pieces
16 medium beets
2 tablespoons red wine vinegar
Juice of 2 lemons
1 cup strong vegetable or beef broth, or more if necessary
1 tablespoon prepared horseradish
1 cup sour cream
Salt and freshly ground pepper to taste
Sour cream for garnish
Chopped fresh dill for garnish

Place onion pieces in a large saucepan and cover with water. Bring to a boil, reduce heat, and simmer, covered, until soft, about 10 minutes. Drain. Trim beets of their tops and scrub carefully. Place beets in a saucepan, add water to cover, and simmer until soft, about 40 minutes. Run under cold water to cool, then peel off skin. Cut beets into quarters and place in the bowl of a food processor fitted with a steel blade. Add onions, vinegar, lemon juice, broth, and horseradish. Puree until smooth. Add sour cream, salt, and pepper and puree. Mixture may be thinned to desired consistency with additional broth. Chill at least 5 hours, or overnight.

Pour into chilled serving bowls and garnish with a dollop of sour cream and a sprinkling of dill.
Serves 10 to 12.

CURRIED EGG SALAD

This makes a tasty sandwich with watercress or arugula on rye or whole-wheat nut bread.

6 hard-boiled eggs, peeled and chopped
2 tablespoons minced onions
2 tablespoons minced celery
1 tablespoon dry mustard
¼ cup dressing, made by mixing equal parts plain yogurt and mayonnaise plus 1 teaspoon curry powder

Place all ingredients in a bowl and toss lightly until well blended.
Serves 6.

SWEET FINALE TOFFEE BARS

These are delicious served with a scoop of ice cream.

1 cup (2 sticks) butter, softened
1 cup brown sugar, firmly packed
1 egg
2 cups sifted cake flour
¼ teaspoon salt
1 12-ounce bag chocolate chips
1 teaspoon vanilla extract

Cream butter and sugar together in a large bowl. Beat in egg, flour, and salt. Stir in chips and vanilla. Spread batter in greased 9 × 9-inch pan. Bake in a preheated 350-degree oven for 25 minutes. Take care not to over-bake. Bars should be very moist, not cakelike. Remove from oven and cool in pan. Cut into squares.
Makes 12 bars.

SPECIAL SALAD DRESSING

This dressing is intended to go over small whole beets, but fresh green beans could be substituted with the same wonderful results.

1 teaspoon salt
Freshly ground pepper to taste
1 tablespoon Dijon mustard
2 to 3 tablespoons red wine vinegar
3 tablespoons olive oil
2 tablespoons hazelnut or walnut oil

Whisk all ingredients together.
Makes ½ cup.

CHICKEN SALAD WITH GRAPES

The grapes and snow peas give a pretty look while also giving good taste and a little crunch.

5 pounds skinless and boneless chicken breasts
2 cups snow peas or sugar snap peas, whichever are crunchier
¾ cup thinly sliced red onions
¾ cup red seedless grape halves
1 cup whole fresh basil leaves, cut into chiffonade*
1 to 1½ cups mayonnaise
Fresh lemon juice to taste
Salt to taste
¼ teaspoon freshly ground black pepper
3 sprigs fresh basil for garnish

Place chicken breasts in a large saucepan. Cover with water and bring to a slow boil. Cover and poach the chicken breasts for 15 minutes, or un-

til cooked through. Let the chicken cool in the liquid, then drain.

Cut the chicken into 1-inch cubes and place in a large mixing bowl. Drop peas into boiling water and cook until color turns bright green, about 10 seconds. Drain and rinse with cold water. Pat dry. Cut the onion slices in half, to make crescent-shaped rings, then add them to the chicken along with the grapes, peas, and basil leaves. Add mayonnaise, mixing gently but thoroughly with your hands. Add lemon juice, salt, and pepper. Garnish with sprigs of fresh basil.

Serves 8 to 10.

* Roll several basil leaves together lengthwise. Slice horizontally as thinly as possible. Doesn't discolor and looks pretty!

AMANDA'S DOGGIE TREATS

This cheese-ball treat for dogs contains nutritious ingredients and just enough cheese to put them on their best behavior.

The one shortcoming of this recipe: people like these treats too!

½ cup grated cheddar cheese
½ cup cottage cheese
2 tablespoons vegetable oil
½ teaspoon salt
¾ cup flour
½ cup fine granola, without raisins, or wheat germ

Combine cheeses, oil, and salt in a large bowl. Add flour gradually, incorporating it with other ingredients until dough sticks together. Shape into small balls the size of large marbles and roll in granola or wheat germ before placing on a lightly greased cookie sheet. Bake in a preheated 350-degree oven for 15 to 20 minutes, or until browned. Cool and store in an airtight container.

Makes 30 treats.

NORTHERN WHITE BEAN SALAD

The dressing that goes over the beans is wonderful warm or cold. And it's equally delicious poured over greens.

1 pound great northern or other white beans, soaked in cold water overnight
1 cup finely chopped Bermuda onion
2 tablespoons vegetable oil
1 cup olive oil
2 tablespoons champagne honey mustard or 1 tablespoon Dijon mustard mixed with 1 tablespoon honey
2 tablespoons orange juice
2 tablespoons tarragon vinegar
1 teaspoon celery seeds (optional)
Salt and freshly ground pepper to taste
1 cup chopped red bell pepper
1 cup chopped zucchini

Drain beans from their soaking liquid and transfer to a large stock pot. Add three parts of fresh water to one part beans. Simmer, covered, approximately two hours, or until tender but still firm. Drain and cool.

Sauté onion quickly in vegetable oil until soft. Remove from heat and set aside. Whisk together olive oil, mustard, orange juice, vinegar, and seasonings. Pour over onions and heat thoroughly. Set aside while you add the pepper and zucchini to beans. Then pour heated onion mixture over beans and vegetables. Blend to incorporate. Salad will be slightly warm. Serve immediately, or at room temperature.

Serves 14.

SPIRITED CHOCOLATE-CHIP COOKIES

½ cup (1 stick) butter, softened
1 cup dark brown sugar, firmly packed
1 egg
2 tablespoons Kahlúa liqueur
1⅛ cups flour
½ teaspoon salt
½ teaspoon baking soda
2 tablespoons unsweetened cocoa
½ cup chopped nuts
1 cup semisweet chocolate chips

Cream butter and sugar together in a large mixing bowl. Add egg and liqueur and beat until smooth. Combine dry ingredients together and add to batter, blending well. Stir in nuts and chips. Drop by generous spoonfuls onto a greased cookie sheet. Bake in a preheated 375-degree oven for 10 minutes, or until lightly browned. Transfer to wire rack to cool.

Makes approximately 18 cookies.

MOIST APPLESAUCE CHUNKIES

½ cup (1 stick) butter, softened
¾ cup brown sugar, firmly packed
¼ cup granulated sugar
1 egg
1 tablespoon molasses
1 cup applesauce
2 cups plus 2 tablespoons flour
1 teaspoon baking soda
¼ teaspoon salt
1 teaspoon cinnamon
1 teaspoon freshly grated nutmeg
½ teaspoon ground cloves
1 cup raisins
½ cup chopped dried apricots
½ cup chopped walnuts

Cream butter with the sugars, egg, and molasses. Add applesauce. Combine dry ingredients in a large bowl and add to batter. Beat until smooth. Add raisins, apricots, and nuts. Drop by generous spoonfuls onto a greased cookie sheet. Bake in a preheated 375-degree oven for 10 to 15 minutes, or until lightly browned. Transfer to wire rack to cool.

Makes approximately 24 cookies.

EASY ROSEMARY FOCACCIA

This bread is traditionally round but can be made in a rectangular shape as well. Rosemary may be added to the dough as well as sprinkled on top.

2¹⁄₈ teaspoons (1 package) active dry yeast
¼ teaspoon sugar
1 cup warm water
½ teaspoon salt
  Approximately 3 cups flour
  Freshly ground pepper to taste
  Approximately 3 tablespoons olive oil
  Cornmeal
  Kosher salt
  Fresh rosemary leaves

In a large bowl, mix yeast and sugar with ¼ cup of warm water. Let sit 5 minutes, until yeast begins to foam. Stir in remaining water. Add ½ teaspoon salt and a generous amount of pepper. Stir in 2½ cups of flour, ½ cup at a time, until dough sticks together and you can form it into a ball. Add more flour if necessary.

Sprinkle your work surface with flour and knead dough ball for about 7 minutes. Then brush the ball with oil, place in a mixing bowl, and cover with a clean towel. Place covered bowl in a warm, draft-free place. Let sit until dough doubles in size, about 2½ to 3 hours.

Preheat oven to 400 degrees.

Punch down dough ball and knead briefly. Then sprinkle a uniform dusting of cornmeal on an oven paddle or cookie sheet. Place dough on paddle or cookie sheet and roll it into a 10-to-12-inch circle at least ½-inch thick. Work the dough gently with your fingertips to distribute evenly toward edges. Prick circle all over with a fork, then brush with oil. Sprinkle with salt and rosemary.

Slide circle onto a pizza pan, baking stone, or another cookie sheet. Bake in a preheated oven until golden brown, about 15 minutes. Serve hot.

Serves 4 to 5.

E.G.H. PASTA

When the tomatoes are ripe at the farm stand, the time is right for this dish, which is a real boon for garlic fans. Those preferring a more subtle flavor may wish to decrease the quantity or chop the cloves finely.

  6 large ripe tomatoes
  8 cloves garlic, thinly sliced
  1 cup plus 3 tablespoons coarsely chopped fresh basil
    Approximately 1½ cups extra-virgin olive oil
½ teaspoon crushed red pepper flakes
1½ pounds fusilli
  1 cup grated mozzarella cheese
    Salt to taste
½ cup grated fresh Parmesan cheese

Cut the tomatoes into wedges, then cut each wedge into thirds. Place wedges in a large glass or ceramic bowl and add garlic and 1 cup basil. Cover tomatoes with olive oil. Add pepper flakes and let mixture sit, covered, in refrigerator for at least 4 hours, or overnight.

Bring a large pot of water to a rolling boil. Add pasta and cook approximately 10 minutes, until *al dente*. Drain and transfer to a large serving bowl. Add mozzarella to hot pasta and toss. Add tomatoes with their marinade and toss again lightly. Add salt, and top with remaining basil and Parmesan cheese. May be served warm, at room temperature, or cold.

Serves 4.

OLD-FASHIONED LEMON-ALMOND SUGAR COOKIES

1 cup (2 sticks) unsalted butter, softened

3 cups confectioners' sugar

¼ teaspoon lemon extract

¼ teaspoon almond extract

1½ teaspoons grated lemon rind

¾ cup blanched slivered almonds

¾ teaspoon salt

1¾ to 2 cups flour

In a large mixing bowl, cream butter with ½ cup sugar until fluffy; add lemon and almond extracts, lemon rind, nuts, and salt and stir until well blended. Add flour and blend until mixture forms a soft dough. Cover with plastic wrap and refrigerate for at least 5 hours, or overnight.

Remove dough from refrigerator and let sit at room temperature for 15 minutes. Form dough into ¾-inch round balls and place at least 1 inch apart on a cookie sheet that has been lined with aluminum foil, shiny side down. Flatten balls slightly with the palm of your hand. Bake in the upper third of a preheated 375-degree oven for 12 to 15 minutes, until bottoms of cookies are slightly golden.

While cookies are baking, sift remaining sugar onto a platter. Remove cookies from oven and allow to cool in pan about three minutes. Press cookies into sugar on both sides and place on a rack to cool completely.

Roll cooled cookies in sugar once more and place in an airtight container. Cookies can be made up to three days in advance of serving.

Makes about 24 cookies.

ASPARAGUS-STUFFED CHICKEN BREASTS WITH PROSCIUTTO AND GOAT CHEESE

4 tablespoons cider vinegar

1 tablespoon honey

⅓ cup coarse-grained mustard

¾ cup olive oil

3 boneless skinless chicken breasts (preferably free range), pounded to ½-inch thickness

6 medium-thin slices prosciutto

¼ pound blue-veined or plain goat cheese, divided into six portions

18 small asparagus spears, trimmed to 5-inch lengths and parboiled

Whisk together the vinegar, honey, mustard, and oil until all ingredients are fully incorporated.

Halve the chicken breasts and lightly brush each half with the vinaigrette. Place a slice of prosciutto on one breast half lengthwise. In one corner, place a portion of goat cheese and three asparagus spears. Roll into a

bundle and tie securely with two 6-inch lengths of twine, each approximately 1½ inches from an end. Trim excess twine. Brush generously with the vinaigrette and repeat with remaining breasts.

Cook on a medium-hot grill, turning on all sides, until done, about 20 minutes.

Serves 6.

FLAVORED HERB BUTTER

Flavoring butter is simple to do and, served in small ramekins, adds panache to any meal.

½ cup (1 stick) unsalted butter, softened

1 tablespoon chopped fresh dill

1 tablespoon chopped fresh thyme

1 tablespoon chopped fresh parsley

Combine butter and herbs in a food processor or mix by hand until ingredients are blended thoroughly and mixture reaches a smooth consistency. Spread into individual ramekins and chill before serving.

Variations: Instead of herbs, you may substitute any of the following flavors by adding them to the same amount of sweet butter:

2 tablespoons anchovy paste

2 tablespoons cracked black peppercorns

2 tablespoons finely chopped black olives

4 cloves garlic, blanched and mashed*

* To blanch garlic, peel cloves and place in a small saucepan of water. Bring to a boil. Remove from heat, drain, and rinse. Repeat process at least one more time. Mash softened cloves and add to butter. The blanching process keeps the garlic from overpowering the butter.

SPICY TUNA TARTARE

Serve this appetizer on small pieces of toast or in a bowl with the toast on the side.

1 pound very fresh fillet of raw tuna
3 tablespoons olive oil
Pinch chopped fresh ginger
4 scallions, minced
4 dashes Tabasco sauce
4 teaspoons cayenne pepper
Pinch white pepper
Fresh lemon juice to taste

Chop tuna into small cubes, then add remaining ingredients except the lemon juice. When satisfied with the seasoning, add the lemon juice little by little. (Be careful not to add too much lemon juice or the acidity will cook the fish.)

Serves 6 to 8.

LEMON SHRIMP

This dish looks especially appealing served in a big glass bowl, with seafood picks or fancy toothpicks nearby.

2 pounds unpeeled green (raw) shrimp
2 tablespoons white wine vinegar
Bouquet garni*
VINAIGRETTE
6 tablespoons olive oil
1 tablespoon white wine vinegar
1 tablespoon Dijon mustard
1 tablespoon celery seed
2 cloves garlic, crushed
½ cup sliced pitted black olives
1 red onion, thinly sliced
1 lemon, thinly sliced
Salt and pepper to taste
Juice of 1 lemon

Peel and devein shrimp. Bring a large kettle of water to a rolling boil. Add the shrimp, vinegar, and bouquet garni and reduce heat to a simmer. Cook for 5 minutes, until shrimp are pink but not tightly curled. Drain immediately.

Meanwhile, prepare the vinaigrette by whisking together all ingredients until fully blended. Pour this over the shrimp, cover, and marinate overnight. Stir in the remaining ingredients just before serving. May be served at room temperature or cold.

Serves 8.

* *Make a bouquet garni by combining 1 bay leaf, 2 to 3 sprigs fresh parsley, and 2 to 3 sprigs fresh thyme in a square of cheesecloth. Tie the corners together tightly with string.*

ROQUEFORT-YOGURT PUREE *EN ENDIVE*

8 ounces Roquefort cheese
1 pint yogurt cheese*
Pinch pepper
1 tablespoon heavy cream (optional)
6 heads endive, separated into leaves

Chill all ingredients thoroughly before beginning. Then, in the bowl of a food processor with the motor running, combine yogurt cheese, Roquefort, and pepper. Puree until smooth. Add cream to thin, if desired. Spread a teaspoon of the mixture on each endive leaf and serve.

Serves 25 to 35 as an hors d'oeuvre.

* *To make yogurt cheese, place 1 quart plain yogurt in a strainer lined with a double layer of cheesecloth and set over a bowl. Let drain 8 hours. Discard the drained material (whey). One quart yogurt will yield 1 pint yogurt cheese.*

MOCK FOIE GRAS

This paté, which has a wonderful hint of ginger, can also be served hot as an entree.

1 pound ground veal
1 pound ground beef chuck
1 pound ground cooked ham
  (preferably smoked)
1 tablespoon butter
½ cup chopped onions
2 tablespoons minced shallots
1 teaspoon minced garlic
1½ cups fresh bread crumbs
½ teaspoon Tabasco sauce
  Salt and pepper to taste
1 tablespoon Cognac
½ cup chopped fresh parsley
2 tablespoons chopped fresh ginger
2 tablespoons chopped fresh dill
½ cup plain yogurt

Combine veal, beef, and ham in a large bowl and mix thoroughly. Melt butter in a skillet and sauté onions, shallots, and garlic over medium heat. Add to meat and stir. Add remaining ingredients and combine thoroughly. Pat mixture into a loaf pan fitted with a draining rack, or place the loaf pan inside a larger pan filled with 1½ inches of boiling water. Bake in a preheated 400-degree oven for 40 to 45 minutes. Let rest in pan 15 minutes before serving.

Serves 25 to 30 people as an hors d'oeuvre; serves 18 as an entree.

ORANGE SPICE TEA

Hot or cold, this is a real lift.

7 bags of mild-flavored tea, such as Irish breakfast, orange pekoe, or Earl Grey
2 small cinnamon sticks
1 teaspoon whole cloves
½ teaspoon ground allspice
1 dozen or more fresh mint leaves
1 cup strained freshly squeezed orange juice
  Juice of 1 lemon
  Sugar or honey to taste

In a saucepan, bring two quarts of water to a boil. Remove from heat and add tea bags and spices. Cover and let steep for 10 minutes. Strain into pitcher and add juices and honey or sugar. Serve hot or add ice.

Makes 2½ quarts.

SMOKED SALMON AND LEEK FRITTATA

These little "egg pies" are a wonderful brunch or luncheon dish.

12 eggs
¼ cup heavy cream
4 teaspoons olive oil
4 ounces smoked salmon, chopped
4 leeks, including ½ inch of green part, chopped
4 teaspoons grated Parmesan cheese

Place eggs, cream, and oil in a bowl and beat until ingredients are well incorporated. Butter 4 4-inch ramekins. Combine salmon and leeks in a separate bowl and divide mixture in half. Beat half the salmon mixture into the egg mixture and pour into ramekins. Spoon the remaining salmon mixture on top of the frittatas and sprinkle with cheese. Place ramekins on a sheet pan and bake in a preheated 375-degree oven for 25 minutes, until the frittata has completely puffed and the center is firm to the touch.

Serves 4.

MARINATED CHERRY TOMATOES

This quick dressing of basil and green peppercorns can be used on many salads, but it gives tomatoes—large and small—a special zing.

1 clove garlic, peeled
2 cups loosely packed fresh basil leaves
1 large egg
1 teaspoon green-peppercorn Dijon mustard
4 teaspoons fresh lemon juice
¾ cup light vegetable oil (preferably canola)
½ cup extra-virgin olive oil
2 pints cherry tomatoes
½ cup chopped fresh parsley for garnish

In a food processor, finely mince the garlic. Add the basil, egg, mustard, and lemon juice and puree. With the motor running, slowly add the oils in a steady stream until mixture is creamy and thick.

Drop cherry tomatoes in boiling water—a few at a time—for a few seconds only. Remove with a slotted spoon, run under cold water, and quickly peel off skins. Repeat until all tomatoes are skinless. Place peeled tomatoes in a deep serving bowl. Pour dressing over tomatoes and marinate in refrigerator at least 4 hours. Sprinkle with chopped parsley and serve. (Or lift tomatoes out of dressing, arrange on individual serving plates, and garnish with chopped parsley.)

Serves 8.

BAREFOOT CONTESSA TURKEY BREAST WITH SPINACH STUFFING

SPINACH STUFFING
1 tablespoon olive oil
¾ cup minced onions
1 teaspoon minced garlic
1 10-ounce package frozen spinach, thawed and well drained
1 egg
½ cup crumbled feta cheese
¼ teaspoon salt
¼ teaspoon pepper

1 5-to-6-pound fresh turkey breast, boned, with skin
3 tablespoons unsalted butter, melted
¼ teaspoon salt
⅛ teaspoon pepper
1 teaspoon each dried basil, oregano, and thyme

Heat the olive oil in a skillet, add onions, and sauté until transparent. Add the garlic and sauté 3 minutes more. Remove from heat. Press excess water out of the spinach with your hands and transfer to a large bowl. Add sautéed vegetables, egg, cheese, salt, and pepper. Mix well.

Lay the turkey breast flat, skin side down, on a cutting board and spread with stuffing. Roll one long side of the turkey breast toward the other to enclose the stuffing and tie with butcher's twine. Place the stuffed breast seam side down on a baking pan. Brush with butter and sprinkle with salt, pepper, and herbs. Roast in a preheated 350-degree oven for 1½ hours, or until internal temperature reaches 140 degrees. Cool and slice.

Serves 12 to 15.

INA'S BREAD PUDDING

This is a delicious finale to a memorable meal, from The Barefoot Contessa in East Hampton, New York.

1 cup raisins
½ cup Grand Marnier liqueur
6 croissants or 2 loaves French bread
3 whole eggs
8 egg yolks
2 teaspoons vanilla extract
1½ cups sugar
5 cups half-and-half
Confectioners' sugar and fresh whole berries for garnish

Combine raisins and liqueur in a medium bowl and allow to soak overnight. The next day, cut the croissants in half or bread loaves into ½-inch slices and arrange half of them in the bottom of an 8 × 14-inch oval Pyrex baking dish. Drain raisins and spread on top of the bread slices, then top with the remaining bread.

Beat together the eggs, yolks, vanilla, sugar, and half-and-half until mixture is thick and golden yellow. Pour over the bread and raisins in the casserole. Weight down the top layer of bread in the liquid with a clean, heavy bowl or plate. Allow to soak for ½ hour. Remove weight and place the Pyrex dish inside a larger pan filled with hot water and bake in a preheated 325-degree oven for 1 hour, or until the custard is set in the middle. Cool. Sift confectioners' sugar over pudding and garnish with berries.

Serves 8 to 10.

WILD RICE SALAD WITH AVOCADO AND TAHINI DRESSING

1 16-ounce package Wehani wild rice*
1 large avocado, peeled
1 clove garlic, peeled
¼ cup tahini
¼ cup extra-virgin olive oil
1 tablespoon tamari
¼ cup rice wine vinegar
Juice of 1 lemon
Pinch cayenne pepper
12 cherry tomatoes, halved
2 scallions, chopped
Chopped parsley for garnish

Cook rice according to package directions. Meanwhile, dice avocado into ½-inch pieces, sprinkle with a bit of lemon juice, and set aside.

Combine garlic, tahini, oil, tamari, vinegar, remaining lemon juice, and cayenne in a food processor and puree. While the machine is running, add oil in a slow, thin stream. Puree until slightly thickened.

Place the rice, avocado, tomatoes, and scallions in a serving bowl and toss lightly with the dressing.

Serves 6.

* A nutty-flavored rice available in most health-food stores.

CUCUMBERS WITH YOGURT-DILL DRESSING

1 large English cucumber
¼ cup chopped Vidalia onion
1 tablespoon chopped fresh mint
1 tablespoon chopped cilantro
⅓ cup plain yogurt
Juice of 1 lemon
Salt and freshly ground pepper to taste

Peel and slice the cucumber thinly. Place in a large bowl with remaining ingredients. Toss lightly and chill for 1 hour before serving.

Serves 4.

GRILLED SWORDFISH STEAKS WITH RED PEPPER SAUCE

The robust taste of the fish marinade is enhanced by charcoal grilling. The red pepper sauce is also an excellent accompaniment for chicken.

2 fresh swordfish steaks, each about ¾ pound and 1¼ inches thick
2 tablespoons tamari
Juice of 1 lime
1 teaspoon rice wine vinegar
1 tablespoon dark sesame oil
4 slices peeled fresh ginger
1 large clove garlic, crushed

RED PEPPER SAUCE
4 tablespoons extra-virgin olive oil
2 large cloves garlic, chopped
2 large red bell peppers, roasted and peeled
Juice of 1 lemon
Salt and freshly ground pepper to taste

Place swordfish steaks side by side in a glass or ceramic baking dish. Blend together tamari, lime juice, vinegar, sesame oil, ginger, and crushed garlic and pour over swordfish, turning the steaks to coat. Cover and refrigerate for at least 1 but no more than 6 hours.

Meanwhile, prepare the sauce: heat olive oil in a small skillet and sauté garlic briefly. Place in food processor with red peppers and lemon juice. Process until mixture reaches consistency of thick salsa. Season with salt and pepper and set aside.

Bring swordfish to room temperature. Grill over charcoal or in a preheated broiler for about 5 minutes on each side, basting once or twice with marinade. Serve with heated red pepper sauce on the side.

Serves 4.

GINGER BEETS

2 pounds fresh small whole beets
2 tablespoons honey
1 tablespoon grated fresh ginger
⅓ cup balsamic vinegar
Butter (optional)

Cut the tops off the beets and scrub thoroughly. Place the beets in a steamer insert and set above several inches of simmering water. Cover and steam until tender, about 30 to 40 minutes. Cool slightly and peel.

Mix together the honey, ginger, and vinegar and pour over the warm beets. Toss with butter, if desired, and serve.

Serves 10 to 12 as part of a buffet; serves 6 to 8 as part of a sit-down meal.

SESAME GREEN BEANS

1 pound fresh green beans, trimmed
1½ tablespoons tamari
1 tablespoon sesame oil
1 tablespoon olive oil
1 tablespoon toasted sesame seeds
Pinch cayenne pepper

In a large pot of boiling water, cook the beans for about 5 minutes. Drain and rinse with cold water.

Mix together remaining ingredients and toss with beans.

Serves 6.

MOM'S SUGAR COOKIES

1 cup (2 sticks) butter, softened
1 cup sugar
2 eggs
1 teaspoon lemon extract
¼ cup milk
2½ cups flour
2 teaspoons cream of tartar
1 teaspoon baking soda

ROYAL ICING
1 egg white
1 to 1½ cups sifted confectioners' sugar
Food coloring

Cream butter and sugar together until fluffy. Beat in eggs, one at a time. Add lemon, then milk, and continue mixing.

Sift together dry ingredients and add gradually to butter mixture. Stir with wooden spoon until dough forms a ball. Cover and chill at least 1 hour.

On a floured surface, roll out dough to a thickness of ¼ inch. Using

cookie cutters, cut dough into shapes. Place on a lightly greased cookie sheet and bake in a preheated 350-degree oven for 10 to 15 minutes, or until cookies begin to brown slightly around the edges. Cool on racks while you prepare Royal Icing.

Combine egg white with sugar and mix until smooth. Divide among small bowls and add desired food coloring to each bowl. Spread an even "base" layer of icing onto cooled cookies and allow to set. (While working with the color in one bowl, keep other bowls covered with a damp cloth.)

Once the base on each cookie has hardened, you are ready to pipe additional colorful designs onto your cookies. Fill a pastry bag fitted with a #1-size tip with colored icing and

let your imagination run wild!

To create dots, lines, and other decorative effects, stiffen icing with additional sugar before piping designs on top of the sugar base.

Makes 36 cookies.

GRILLED MIXED SAUSAGES WITH SWEET PEPPERS

Undercooking the vegetables so that they are hot but still crunchy provides a refreshing contrast to the rich and pungent sausages.

Approximately 3 tablespoons olive oil
3 green bell peppers, seeded and cut in half
3 red bell peppers, seeded and cut in half
3 large Spanish onions, peeled and cut in quarters
1 pound kielbasa
1 pound turkey sausage
1 pound Italian sausage
12 to 14 sprigs rosemary

Rub olive oil on vegetables and set aside. Place the sausages on a hot grill and cook, turning frequently, for approximately 10 minutes, or until they begin to brown. Add vegetables and rosemary sprigs to grill and cook for an additional 10 minutes. Sausages should be well browned and vegetables should be cooked but still crunchy. Slice sausages in serving-size pieces before arranging with vegetables on a large serving platter. Add additional fresh sprigs of rosemary for garnish.

Serves 6 to 8.

CENTER-STAGE CHOCOLATE CAKE

¾ cup (1½ sticks) butter, softened
1⅔ cups sugar
3 eggs
1 teaspoon vanilla extract
2 cups flour
¾ cup unsweetened cocoa, or more to taste
1¼ teaspoons baking soda
¼ teaspoon salt
1⅓ cups water
   FROSTING
4 ounces unsweetened chocolate
2 tablespoons butter
½ cup milk
1 16-ounce box confectioners' sugar
1 teaspoon vanilla extract

In a large bowl, combine butter, sugar, eggs, and vanilla. Beat at high speed of electric mixer for 3 minutes. Combine dry ingredients and add alternately with water to the butter mixture. Blend well and pour into two greased 9-inch round baking pans.

Bake in a preheated 350-degree oven for 30 to 35 minutes, or until a cake tester inserted in the center comes out clean. Cool 5 minutes in pans, then turn layers out on a cake rack to cool completely.

Meanwhile, make the frosting: melt the chocolate, butter, and milk in a large saucepan. Stir in sugar and vanilla, mixing thoroughly. Cool. Spread some frosting over the top of one layer of the cooled cake. Top with the other layer and frost the top and sides of the entire cake.

Makes 1 9-inch cake.

NEW POTATOES WITH ROSEMARY

A subtle blending of herbs makes this a memorable dish.

1 pound small new potatoes
3 tablespoons light olive oil
1 tablespoon tarragon vinegar
1 teaspoon Dijon mustard
1 tablespoon anchovy paste
1 clove garlic, crushed
1 teaspoon chopped fresh rosemary or oregano

Peel a narrow strip around the circumference of each potato and boil until just fork tender. Drain. Mix together remaining ingredients and toss with warm potatoes. Serve immediately.

Serves 4.

SOUTHWESTERN SALAD WITH TANGY VINIAGRETTE

⅓ cup tarragon vinegar
2 teaspoons anchovy paste
2 teaspoons Dijon mustard
   Salt and freshly ground pepper to taste
1 teaspoon dried oregano
1 cup olive oil
½ pound young green beans
   Pinch baking soda
3 carrots
3 cold cooked beets
1 cucumber, peeled
1 medium head Bibb lettuce
   Alfalfa sprouts for garnish
   Spears of fresh chive for garnish

Place all dressing ingredients except olive oil in food processor and blend. With the machine still running, slowly add oil in a thin stream until it is fully incorporated and dressing is slightly thickened. Transfer to a serving vessel and set aside.

Blanch beans in boiling water, to which baking soda has been added, for no more than 30 seconds. Drain and rinse under cold water to stop cooking. Beans should still be crisp.

Scrub and grate carrots. Slice beets and cut slices into thin strips. Peel cucumber, then run the prongs of a fork down the sides. Slice cucumber thinly. Wash lettuce leaves and pat dry.

Create small groups of all the vegetables on a serving platter. Arrange sprouts loosely in the center. Decorate with strips of chive. Serve with dressing on the side.

Serves 6.

Variations
•• Substitute raspberry or red wine vinegar for tarragon vinegar.
•• Substitute ⅔ cup oil mixed with ⅓ cup vinegar for 1 cup olive oil.
•• Substitute 1 teaspoon minced garlic for anchovy paste.
•• Garnish with fresh thyme, sage, or other herbs instead of chives.
•• Add 2 teaspoons minced shallots to vinaigrette before blending.
•• Add 1 tablespoon capers to dressing before blending.

ZESTY MELON SALSA

This mild and unusual salsa is good with tortilla chips or as a condiment for chicken or fish. Brave souls may wish to add red pepper flakes, diced jalapeño peppers, and/or more Tabasco sauce to taste.

1 14-ounce can plum tomatoes, well drained
½ cup pineapple juice
¼ cup white wine vinegar
5 cloves garlic, minced
½ teaspoon Tabasco sauce
Juice of 2 limes
½ cup chopped cilantro
½ cantaloupe, peeled and cut in bite-size pieces
¼ honeydew melon, peeled and cut in bite-size pieces
1 medium red onion, finely diced
1 red bell pepper, finely diced

Puree tomatoes in food processor. Add pineapple juice, vinegar, garlic, Tabasco, lime juice, and cilantro and process 2 to 3 seconds more. Pour tomato puree into a large serving bowl and stir in the chopped melon and vegetables.

Serves 15.

STUFFED POTATO CHOICES

Scrub baking potatoes carefully and prick skin several times with a fork. Bake in a preheated 400-degree oven for 50 to 60 minutes. Remove from oven and cut a slit down the middle of each potato, leaving an inch or so at either end. Push ends together so potato flesh loosens and comes to the surface. Stuff and garnish as desired.

STUFFINGS
Grated cheddar, mozzarella, or blue cheese
Sour cream
Cottage cheese
Yogurt

TOPPINGS
Minced hot peppers
Diced bell peppers
Minced onions, chives, or scallions
Chopped tomatoes
Crumbled bacon
Anchovy strips
Diced cooked ham
Chopped hard-boiled egg

Set out small bowls of the various potato stuffings and let your guests select one or two—or more!

PUMPKIN PEANUT SOUP

This soup could become a "new" Thanksgiving tradition.

1 tablespoon butter
1 cup chopped raw peanuts
2 large cloves garlic, crushed
1 cup finely chopped onion
2 teaspoons freshly grated ginger
1 teaspoon salt
½ teaspoon cinnamon
½ teaspoon ground coriander seeds
¼ teaspoon whole cloves
1 teaspoon ground cumin
¼ teaspoon cayenne pepper
1 14-ounce can chicken broth
½ cup unsalted, unsweetened natural peanut butter
1 tablespoon honey
1 cup canned pumpkin
1¼ cups buttermilk, at room temperature
Slivered orange zest for garnish

Melt butter in a large skillet and add the next four ingredients. Sauté for 5 minutes. Add spices and chicken broth and simmer 10 minutes. Add peanut butter and honey and cook 5 minutes more. Remove from heat.

In a food processor, puree the soup in batches until creamy. Transfer to a large soup pot and whisk in pumpkin and buttermilk. Stir over medium-low heat until steamy. Transfer to a tureen and garnish with slivers of orange zest.

Serves 6.

SWEDISH GLÖGG

This is a spirited Scandinavian punch that is a traditional part of the Christmas holidays.

1 cup Burgundy wine
1 cup dry or sweet sherry
½ cup sweet vermouth
1 cup vodka
¼ to ½ jigger Angostura bitters
1 stick cinnamon
¼ teaspoon cardamom, or more to taste
½ cup raisins
½ cup blanched slivered almonds

Combine all ingredients except raisins and almonds in a saucepan and heat gently. Just before serving, add raisins and almonds, or divide raisins and almonds among 8 serving cups and pour in hot glögg.

Serves 8.

PRESERVED EGGPLANT

Serve as a first course, drizzled with hot oil and tossed with roasted red pepper strips, or chop and use as a topping for pizza or pasta.

> *4 to 5 medium-sized eggplants (about*
> *5 pounds), cut in ½-inch slices*
> *⅓ cup coarse sea salt*
> *6 cups white wine vinegar*
> *4 cups extra-virgin olive oil*
> *4 teaspoons whole coriander seeds*
> *8 dried hot chilies*

Toss eggplant slices with salt in a large bowl. Spread eggplant evenly on layers of paper towels. Cover with another layer of paper towels and weigh down with a cutting board or heavy baking sheet. Let drain for at least 1 hour.

Bring vinegar to a boil in a large saucepan, add eggplant slices, and bring back to a boil. Simmer 5 minutes. Drain slices and pat dry with paper towels. At this point you may leave the eggplant in slices or cut each slice into quarters for a chunkier presentation.

In each of 4 sterilized 1-pint mason jars, pour about ½ inch of oil. Divide eggplant among the jars, add 1 teaspoon coriander seeds and two chopped chilies to each jar, and fill with remaining oil.

Seal and store in a cool place at least one week before serving. After opening, add more oil to cover eggplants.

Makes 4 pints.

CHOCOLATE NUT COOKIES

These can be made up to a week before serving and kept in an airtight container.

> *1 cup (2 sticks) unsalted butter,*
> *softened*
> *½ cup brown sugar, firmly packed*
> *½ cup granulated sugar*
> *¼ cup molasses*
> *2 eggs*
> *1 teaspoon vanilla extract*
> *2½ cups flour*
> *1 teaspoon baking soda*
> *¼ teaspoon salt*
> *¼ teaspoon freshly grated nutmeg*
> *1½ cups roasted unsalted cashews,*
> *chopped*
> *½ cup chocolate chips*

Cream butter, sugars, and molasses in a large bowl until fluffy. Beat in eggs and vanilla, then mix in dry ingredients. Stir in nuts and chips. Cover and refrigerate at least 1 hour, or overnight.

Place a sheet of aluminum foil shiny side down on a cookie sheet. Drop dough by teaspoonfuls onto the sheet, spacing cookies 2 inches apart. Bake in a preheated 350-degree oven until golden, about 12 minutes. Transfer to a wire rack to cool.

Makes about 36 cookies.

GARLIC-HERB VINEGAR

A pretty vinegar bottle is half the gift!

> *3 large cloves garlic, peeled*
> *Sprigs of fresh herbs such as basil,*
> *oregano, thyme, or lovage, rinsed*
> *and patted dry (approximately*
> *1 cup)*
> *3 cups white-wine or cider vinegar*

Place garlic cloves in bottom of a decorative 1-quart glass bottle. Loosely pack in a small bundle of herbs.

In a large saucepan, heat vinegar until hot, but not boiling. Pour through a funnel over herbs and garlic. Seal with a cork. Allow to stand in a dark cool place for at least 2 weeks.

Makes approximately 4 cups.

BOUNTIFUL BOARD FRENCH TOAST

Vanilla flavoring and rich challah bread make this French toast, created by The Bountiful Board in East Hampton, New York, deliciously different.

> *4 eggs*
> *1 cup milk*
> *4 tablespoons sugar*
> *1 teaspoon vanilla extract*
> *4 1½-inch-thick slices challah bread**
> *Confectioners' sugar*
> *4 tablespoons butter*
> *Maple syrup to taste*

Beat eggs, milk, sugar, and vanilla together. Cut each square of bread on the diagonal, prick with fork, and soak for 1 hour in egg mixture.

Heat griddle or skillet and brush with butter. Sauté bread slices 5 minutes each side, or until golden.

Remove from griddle, sprinkle with sugar, top with a pat of butter, and drizzle maple syrup over the top.

Serves 2.

* For best results, use challah that is at least 2 days old.

EXOTIC GAZPACHO

This classic cold tomato soup is given a Middle Eastern twist with pungent spices.

2 teaspoons paprika
2 teaspoons ground cumin
¼ teaspoon cayenne pepper
4 tablespoons olive oil
1 tablespoon white wine vinegar
1 28-ounce can tomatoes
1 large cucumber, seeded and chopped
1 large red onion, chopped
6 cloves garlic, minced
2 tablespoons fresh lemon juice
½ cup chopped cilantro
¼ cup dry white wine
2 teaspoons kosher salt
1 medium green bell pepper, chopped
4 stalks celery, chopped

In a small saucepan, combine paprika, cumin, cayenne, olive oil, and vinegar. Bring to a boil and cook over medium heat, stirring constantly, for about 3 minutes. Remove from heat and set aside.

Drain the tomatoes, reserving the liquid. In a food processor, puree the tomatoes, half the cucumber, half the onion, the garlic, lemon juice, and cilantro. Add cooled spice mixture and wine and puree again. Thin to desired consistency with reserved tomato liquid. Add salt. Cover and chill at least 4 hours before serving.

Pour into individual serving bowls and garnish with remaining chopped onions, remaining chopped cucumber, and chopped green pepper and celery.

Serves 6.

BEACH CLAMBAKE

12 ears fresh corn, in husks
6 pounds clams
6 pounds mussels
1 tablespoon white vinegar
Approximately 60 small new potatoes
Kosher salt to taste
1½ pounds (6 sticks) butter
½ cup olive oil
Wet seaweed
12 live lobsters, about 1 pound each
4 lemons, cut into wedges

At least 2 hours before guests arrive, dig a 3 × 5 × 2-foot-deep pit in the sand. The bottom and sides of the pit should be lined with bricks, stones, or cinder blocks to keep sand from falling into the pit. Next, fill the pit with charcoal, light, and let burn until very hot white embers remain.

Meanwhile, cut the topmost silk off the ears of corn and soak ears in water for at least 1 hour. This is also a good time to scrub the clams well with a stiff brush under cold water. The mussels should soak in 2 quarts of cold water with 1 tablespoon of white vinegar added for at least 30 minutes. At the end of the soaking time, rinse well with cold water.

About 45 minutes before you are ready to serve your clambake, place grill grates over the pit opening and place two large cast-iron frying pans on the grates. Melt 1 stick butter and ¼ cup oil in each pan. Add potatoes to pans, sprinkle generously with salt, and cook, shaking pans frequently to cook potatoes evenly. Next, drain water off corn and place ears (still in husks) directly on grill. The outside husks will blacken a bit as the corn cooks, but the corn inside remains sweet and moist.

After corn and potatoes have cooked for approximately 15 minutes, layer seaweed on half of the grate area. Split lobster tails on the underside by running a sharp knife along sinew. Then lay lobsters on top of seaweed. Turn lobsters at least twice as they cook.

During the last 20 minutes of cooking, place the mussels and the clams on top of the seaweed. The clams and mussels are done when they open (do not eat any that do not open).

Melt remaining butter in a saucepan on top of grill. Apply with a brush to husked corn, lobsters, and clams. Serve lemon wedges on the side.

Serves 12.

CHERRY TOMATO AND BLUE CHEESE SALAD

1 pint cherry tomatoes
4 ounces blue cheese
4 to 6 scallions, diced
2 tablespoons fresh lemon juice
1 tablespoon olive oil
Freshly ground pepper to taste

Slice tomatoes in half, place in a large serving bowl, and toss with cheese and scallions. Blend lemon juice, oil, and pepper and pour over tomato-cheese mixture. Toss to blend.
Serves 4.

DIANE'S SUGGESTIONS FOR A WELL-STOCKED PANTRY

OILS
Olive — both plain and flavored with sprigs of rosemary, tarragon, or chunks of garlic
Corn
Peanut
Safflower

VINEGARS
Balsamic
Cider — flavored with any of the following: garlic, peppercorns, basil, tarragon, rosemary, dill
Novelty — raspberry, peach
White wine
Red wine

MUSTARDS
Plain Dijon
Herbed — with green peppers, tarragon, or basil
Grainy, in crocks
Honey
Plain American — hot dog type

CHUTNEYS
Silver Palate Mango
Plain Major Grey's

CONDIMENTS
Tomato paste (in tube)
Anchovy paste (in tube)
Horseradish
Soy sauce (light)

BROTH
Chicken bouillon
Beef bouillon

PARMESAN CHEESE
Keep chunks in freezer and grate as needed

DRIED FRUITS AND NUTS
Almonds
Pecans
Walnuts
Raisins

DRIED HERBS AND SPICES
Bay leaf, Dill, Basil, Oregano, Rosemary, Tarragon, Parsley, Curry powder, Chili powder, Nutmeg, Cloves, Cinnamon, Ginger, Salt, Peppercorns (black, white, and pink)

FLAVORED EXTRACTS
Vanilla
Almond
Lemon

BAKING ESSENTIALS
Baking soda, Baking powder, Cornstarch, Cornmeal, Flour, Sugar, Brown sugar, Confectioners' sugar, Dark molasses, Corn syrup, Chocolate chips

CHOCOLATE
Unsweetened
Semisweet
Powdered cocoa

COFFEES
Espresso — regular and decaffeinated
Flavored — Hazelnut, Vanilla Almond, Viennese Cinnamon

TEAS
Apricot
Vanilla

Plum
Earl Grey
Black Currant
Constant Comment

CRACKERS
Carr's basic assortment
Wheat Thins

BEVERAGES
Club soda
Tonic
Evian water
San Pellegrino sparkling water
Bottled Lemon Juice and Lime Juice

Baggies of Ice

LIQUOR
Vodka
Gin
Scotch
Rum
Bourbon
Liqueurs and cordials

WINE
3 bottles of red
3 bottles of white

PASTA AND RICE
Linguini
Rigatoni (dried, in jars)
Tortellini
Ravioli (fresh, in freezer)
White and brown rice

CANDLES
12-inch tapers in white or beige, gold, hunter, bronze, and burgundy
Boxes of votives

FLOWER ARRANGING
Organize the pantry with baskets, vases, containers, boxes, crates, frogs, Spanish moss, packing straw, raffia, white rocks, black Japanese rocks, mini-pinecones, driftwood, florist's tape, and Oasis.

Resources

Shopping for the table is full of surprises. Often, the most useful and unusual items turn up where I least expect them, which makes putting together a tabletop resources section a challenging job. Where to begin? Where to stop?

I have included shops that specialize in or stock a heavy concentration of tabletop or kitchen/dining items. Starting with my own personal favorites, gleaned from travels or friends' suggestions, I made a list. Then I began to network throughout the country. My only regret is the shops I didn't hear about—I look forward to discovering them!

Space limitations required me to exclude many fine antiques stores that frequently carry tabletop treasures. However, many such stores are listed in *Formal Country*.

Happy shopping—and happy entertaining!

ALABAMA

The Elegant Earth
1907 Cahaba Rd.
Birmingham, AL 35223
(205) 870-3264
Garden and home objects such as terra-cotta vessels, hand-painted watering cans, lead and stone garden ornaments, benches, animals, and urns.

ARIZONA

Dos Cabezas
6166 N. Scottsdale Rd., Suite 300
(The Borgata)
Scottsdale, AZ 85253
(602) 991-7004
Mexican tableware, including silverware from Taxco; hand-painted china and porcelain dinnerware; glasses and stemware; folk art and colonial antiques. Also in Phoenix.

CALIFORNIA

Bell'occhio
8 Brady St.
San Francisco, CA 94103
(415) 864-4048
Changing small treasures, including an extensive collection of unusual ribbons; place and menu cards; vintage millinery trims and fruits, and one-of-a-kind furniture.

Candelier
60 Maiden Lane
San Francisco, CA 94108
(415) 989-8600
Vast selection of unusual candles and candle holders, as well as whimsical home accessories such as topiaries, bark and willow objects, plates, and picture frames.

Cookin'
339 Divisadero
San Francisco, CA 94117
(415) 861-1854
Utilitarian and decorative vintage kitchen wares and tableware, including copper bakeware and dessert molds in the forms of animals.

Sue Fisher King
3067 Sacramento St.
San Francisco, CA 94118
(415) 922-7276
Up-scale tableware, including imported flatware and pottery as well as table and bed linens. Items from Sue Fisher King featured in this book include the Siena dinnerware, p. 37; damask napkins, napkin rings, French flatware, and glassware, p. 35; star plates and celestial demitasse cups and saucers, p. 42.

The French Connection
29 N. Santa Cruz Ave.
Los Gatos, CA 95030
(408) 354-2232
Country French antiques, including tables and chairs, as well as home accessories.

The Gardener
1836 Fourth St.
Berkeley, CA 94710
(415) 548-4545
Objects that bring the garden and the home together.

Indigo Seas
123 N. Robertson Blvd.
Los Angeles, CA 90048
(213) 550-8758

Home accessories with the mystery of seaports and sea voyages about them. 1940s vintage tablecloths are available here.

Ireland-Pays
2428 Main St.
Santa Monica, CA 90403
(310) 396-5035

Traditional tableware, including classic creamware, bristol blue glass, and Irish linen place mats, as well as English home accessories.

The Pavilion
148 W. Colorado Blvd.
Pasadena, CA 91105
(818) 792-2956

Design accessories for the home, including tableware (often featuring holiday themes), as well as bath, patio, and garden objects.

Pottery Shack
1212 South Coast Highway
Laguna Beach, CA 92651
(714) 494-1141

Pottery for every room of the house, from outdoor planters to fine table settings, with hand-painted tableware a specialty. The Cottage Rose pattern featured on p. 183 can be found here.

Susan's Store Room
239 San Anselmo Ave.
San Anselmo, CA 94960
(415) 456-1333

A multifaceted collector's shop with tableware and decorative accessories, including 1930s Bauer earthenware and new majolica.

Terra Cotta
11925 Montana Ave.
Los Angeles, CA 90049
(213) 826-7878

Tableware, including new and antique china, pottery, and stoneware as well as linens and garden and gift objects such as topiaries. The Billie Goldsmith Limoges china, p. 15; Della Robbia dinnerware, beige checked place mat, damask napkin, decorative vinegar bottles, and artichoke salt and pepper shakers, p. 14 came from Terra Cotta.

Turner Martin
540 Emerson St.
Palo Alto, CA 94301
(415) 324-8700

Mostly handmade objects, ranging from found-object art and large floral designs to tabletop items.

La Ville du Soleil
444 Post St.
San Francisco, CA 94102
(415) 434-0657

The French look is evident in this shop, featuring white and colorful hand-painted china and porcelain, glassware, linens, doilies, ribbons, and baskets.

Yippie-ei-o!
1308 Montana Ave.
Santa Monica, CA 90403
(213) 451-2520

The West meets the tabletop here, with vintage dishware, cookie jars, tablecloths, and napkins with a cowboy/western motif.

COLORADO

Krismar
508 E. Lionshead Circle
Vail, CO 81657
(303) 476-3603

A wide-ranging tabletop, kitchen, and home-furnishings store, Krismar offers artistic lines of pottery and china, flatware, crystal, linens, high-end cookware, and cookbooks.

CONNECTICUT

Lillian August Collection
17 Main St.
Westport, CT 06880
(203) 454-1775

Tableware, including French, Italian, and Portuguese hand-painted pottery; linens and fabrics; and dining room furniture in international country styles.

The Complete Kitchen
865 Post Rd.
Darien, CT 06820
(203) 655-7355

This kitchenware emporium also features vintage "country" silver made for English and French grand hotels, cafés, and restaurants—from oversized bistro spoons to toast racks to cake stands. Also in Greenwich.

James Dew & Son
1171 Boston Post Rd.
Guilford, CT 06437
(203) 453-3847

Fine handcrafted reproduction eighteenth-century furniture, including handsome dining room tables, chairs, cupboards, and other furniture for the home.

Fishtales Gallery
Route 10 North Riverdale Farms
Avon, CT 06001
(203) 677-2552
Playful contemporary tableware and crafts, including geometric flatware, hand-painted glassware, liner plates, ceramic and pottery bowls, and serving pieces such as salad servers.

Lafalce, Campbell, Robbin
12 Lasalle Rd.
West Hartford, CT 06107
(203) 231-7742
Tabletop and home accessories with an eclectic blend of contemporary and traditional designs. In addition to a complete range of tableware, from napkins to stemware, the shop offers brushed-steel étagères and custom-designed mirrors.

Main St. Cellar Antiques
120 Main St.
New Canaan, CT 06840
(203) 966-8348
Antique china and pottery, including Canton, majolica, lusterware, and yellowware; country and high-country furniture; and vintage quilts, linens, and textiles.

E.G.H. Peter, Inc.
PO Box 52
Norfolk, CT 06058
(203) 542-5221
Antique table and decorative wares, including Minton, redware, and lusterware; unusual painted furniture and wicker pieces.

J. Seitz & Co.
9 E. Shore Rd.
New Preston, CT 06777
(203) 868-0119
Gaily painted New Mexican furniture and other folksy decorative objects for the home and table, including pottery, twig-inspired flatware, and table linens.

Monique Shay Antiques
920 Main St.
Woodbury, CT 06798
(203) 263-3186
French and Canadian antique furniture in painted and natural pine, with a good selection of tables and chairs.

The Silo
44 Upland Rd.
New Milford, CT 06776
(203) 355-0300
Tableware with a country appeal, from Italian spongeware and hand-painted pottery to French jelly glasses.

WASHINGTON, D.C.

Dalton Brody
3412 Idaho Ave. NW
Washington, DC 20016
(202) 244-7197
The tabletop and antiques boutiques within this shop offer an eclectic mix of handcrafted pottery, Limoges, and antique silver, including trays and biscuit barrels.

Jane Wilner
5300 Wisconsin Ave. NW
Washington, DC 20015
(202) 966-1484
Linens for the table, bed, and bath.

FLORIDA

Charlie's Locker
1445 SE 17th St.
Fort Lauderdale, FL 33316
(305) 523-3350
For land- and sea-bound tables, this shop offers everything from rope to tabletop wares, ranging from attractive plastics to fine porcelain, glass, and linens.

GEORGIA

Fragile
175 Mount Vernon Highway
Atlanta, GA 30328
(404) 257-1323
Tabletop objects, many with a contemporary edge, including hand-painted pottery and Limoges, unique stemware and handcrafted art glass, and table linens.

Peridōt
327 Buckhead Ave.
Atlanta, GA 30305
(404) 261-7028
Tableware, including Italian and Portuguese ceramic dinnerware, hand-blown glassware, and linens, as well as furniture and garden items.

Charles Willis
465 E. Paces Ferry Rd.
Atlanta, GA 30305
(404) 233-9487
Over one hundred patterns in china and ceramic dinnerware are available here, as well as silver and crystal.

ILLINOIS

Adesso
600 Central Ave.
Highland Park, IL 60035
(708) 433-8525
Tableware and accessories for the home, most hand made by artisans.

City Source
28 E. Huron
Chicago, IL 60611
(312) 664-5499
Home furnishings with an emphasis on natural materials and handcrafted objects, including natural linens, decorative bowls and glass objects, and gourmet food items.

Material Possessions
54 E. Chestnut St.
Chicago, IL 60011
(312) 280-4885
Design-oriented tableware, ranging from complete place settings with table accessories to eclectic decorative objects. Also in Winnetka.

KANSAS

Plaid Giraffe
302 N. Rock Rd.
Wichita, KS 67206
(316) 683-1364
Everything for a well-dressed table, including pottery and china, stemware, silverware, cookbooks, and French and English country antiques.

LOUISIANA

As You Like It
3025 Magazine St.
New Orleans, LA 70115
(504) 897-6915 and (800) 828-2311
A wide selection of sterling flatware, including heavy "estate" silver and hollowware.

Lucullus
610 Chartres St.
New Orleans, LA 70130
(504) 528-9620
Culinary antiques, art, and objects arranged in room settings.

MAINE

Edgecomb Potters
Route 27
Edgecomb, ME 04556
(207) 882-6802
An American crafts gallery featuring handcrafted porcelain dinnerware, functional pottery, and art pottery.

The Farm
Mildram Rd.
Wells, ME 04090
(207) 985-2656
English antiques for the more formal table, including silver serving pieces such as fish sets with pearl handles, cut glassware, fine tables, sideboards, and other furniture.

Maine Cottage Furniture
Lower Falls Landing, Route 88
Yarmouth, ME 04096
(207) 846-1430
Cottage-inspired furniture and accessories, including octagonal and lattice dining tables in bright finishes, as well as tableware such as hand-painted pottery, linens, and candles.

Sheepscot River Pottery
Route 1
Edgecomb, ME 04556
(207) 882-9410
Representing over two hundred American crafts people, this studio/showroom features a complete line of decorative porcelain and stoneware. Also in Wiscasset.

MARYLAND

Urban Country
7801 Woodmont Ave.
Bethesda, MD 20814
(301) 654-0500
This light and airy store is filled with furniture (much of it antique pine) and home accessories, including tableware.

MASSACHUSETTS

Lacoste Gallery
39 Thoreau St.
Concord, MA 01742
(508) 369-0278
Functional and decorative American crafts, including handcrafted tableware in china, earthenware, stoneware, and porcelain; hand-blown stemware; and quilts and pillows.

La Ruche
168 Newbury St.
Boston, MA 02116
(617) 536-6366
A fanciful collection of tableware, including colorful dinnerware, hand-painted stemware, linens, and other decorative accessories, as well as country and painted furniture.

Marcoz
177 Newbury St.
Boston, MA 02116
(617) 262-0780
Antique French, English, and American decorative furnishings and accessories, including unusual tableware.

Pinch Pottery and the Ferrin Gallery
179 Main Street
Northampton, MA 01060
(413) 586-4509
A retail store and an American crafts gallery under one roof, featuring handcrafted ceramic dinnerware and serving pieces.

MICHIGAN

Huzza
136 E. Main St.
Harbor Springs, MI 49740
(616) 526-2128
A sophisticated mix of antiques, home accessories, and tabletop objects such as hand-painted pottery, fine china, glassware, and linens.

MISSOURI

Portobello and Camel
1708 W. 45th St.
Kansas City, MO 64111
(816) 931-2280
Antique tableware, from vintage white linens and lots of blue-and-white china to silver and plated tea sets and flatware.

NEW JERSEY

Earthly Pleasures
610 North Maple Ave.
Ho Ho Kus, NJ 07423
(201) 444-4834
Tableware, including glass, clay, and stoneware plates and serving pieces; china; hand-blown glassware; and American crafts.

Handmaids
37 Maple St.
Summit, NJ 07091
(908) 273-0707
Handmade pottery, including bowls, platters, and pitchers; hand-blown glassware; tablecloths and place mats; and some vintage tableware.

The Sampler
96 Summit Ave.
Summit, NJ 07901
(908) 277-4747
Decorative accessories for the home, including hand-painted furniture and objects, dried arrangements, and handcrafted gifts and collectibles. The painted watering can featured on p. 163 came from this shop.

NEW MEXICO

The Chile Shop
109 E. Water St.
Santa Fe, NM 87501
(505) 983-6080
Southwestern tableware, including unusual items such as gourd food warmers and pottery tortilla steamers, as well as pottery dinnerware, etched glassware, linens, and wooden salad servers in the shapes of cacti, coyotes, and snakes.

Hand Maiden
Shelby at Water St.
Santa Fe, NM 87501
(505) 982-8368
Functional and decorative pottery made locally by at least 25 potters, with a broad range of colors and styles.

NEW YORK CITY

ABC Carpet and Home
888 Broadway
New York, NY 10003
(212) 473-3000
Table and home accessories ranging from colorful earthenware plates and bowls to an extensive collection of table linens. Dining room furniture in many styles, antique and new, is available on another floor.

Barneys New York
106 Seventh Ave.
New York, NY 10011
(212) 929-9000
Distinctive tableware and home accessories, including hand-painted plates and platters, flatware, glass, and stemware; serving items; and an extensive table-linens collection.

Casa Maia Antiques and Decorative Arts
1143 Park Ave.
New York, NY 10128
(212) 534-3615
Unique decorative furnishings and accessories, including topiary and other dried-flower arrangements.

Ceramica
59 Thompson St.
New York, NY 10012
(800) 228-0858 and (212) 941-1307
Hand-painted Italian ceramic tableware, from complete place settings with accessory pieces to one-of-a-kind decorative pieces.

Dampierre & Co.
79 Greene St.
New York, NY 10012
(212) 966-1357
Distinctive objects for the home, ranging from painted furniture to tableware such as hand-painted linens and wire baskets.

Le Fanion
299 W. Fourth St.
New York, NY 10014
(800) 258-8760
Traditional pottery made by French artisans as well as antique furniture and decorative accessories.

Laura Fisher Antiques
1050 Second Ave. #57A
New York, NY 10022
(212) 838-2596
Antique American textiles and linens, quilts, rugs, and folk art.

Fishs Eddy
889 Broadway
New York, NY 10003
(212) 420-9020
Sturdy tableware—either vintage or produced using original molds—from clubs, yachts, schools, and restaurants. Pieces include pitchers, platters, plates, and mugs—many with crests and logos. The hotel dinnerware, p. 194, came from this store. Also at 551 Hudson St.

Gordon Foster
1322 Third Ave.
New York, NY 10021
(212) 744-4922
Artful decorative pieces, including contemporary American pottery, a selection of unusual vases and bowls.

Patricia Funt Gallery
50½ E. Seventy-eighth St.
New York, NY 10021
(212) 772-2482
Whimsical objects such as Victorian alphabet plates, antique animal figures, and other small accessories.

James II Galleries
15 E. Fifty-seventh St.
New York, NY 10022
(212) 355-7040
For the highly decorated table, eighteenth- and nineteenth-century decorative objects, including Victorian colored glass and silverplate.

Robert Homma William Lipton
27 E. Sixty-first St.
New York, NY 10021
(212) 593-4341
Original and eclectic home and table accessories ranging from antique Ming porcelain to lovely French ribbons.

Sura Kayla SoHo
484 Broome St.
New York, NY 10013
(212) 941-8757
Custom floral compositions, artful topiaries, and other decorative small objects for the home and tabletop.

Keesal & Mathews
1244 Madison Ave.
New York, NY 10128
(212) 410-1800
Tabletop and home accessories, ranging from hand-painted plates and stemware to fanciful candle sticks, picture frames, and lamps. Also in East Hampton, NY.

Kitschen
15 Christopher St.
New York, NY 10014
(212) 727-0430
Secondhand vintage items for the kitchen and table, including bottle-green glassware, pitchers, sets of glasses, and picnic hampers.

Lexington Gardens
1008 Lexington Ave.
New York, NY 10021
(212) 861-4390
Unique garden-related objects, including nursery pots and moss-covered topiaries, as well as delicate English wire furniture.

Adrien Linford
1320 Madison Ave.
New York, NY 10128
(212) 289-4427
Finely crafted objects for the home and table that are functional and stylish. Wide-ranging table settings include plates, flatware, serving pieces, linens, and small decorative objects. The damask napkins on p. 188 came from this shop.

LS Collection
765 Madison Ave.
New York, NY 10021
(212) 472-3355
Tabletop accessories and objects for the home with contemporary flair.

Frank McIntosh at Henri Bendel
712 Fifth Ave.
New York, NY 10019
(212) 247-1100

Distinctive home and table accessories. The hand-painted napkins and sisal place mats, p. 154; decorative glasses and pitcher, p. 157; champagne flutes, p. 159; and star plates, cocktail napkins, and wooden tray, p. 152, came from this store.

J. Mavec & Co.
625 Madison Ave.
New York, NY 10022
(212) 888-8100

Fine British silver from the Georgian, Victorian, and Edwardian periods.

Charlotte Moss & Co.
1027 Lexington Ave.
New York, NY 10021
(212) 772-3320

Formal English home furnishings, with small tabletop accessories such as place-card holders and salt cellars as well as antique fine china and new French pieces adorned with fruit.

Pantry & Hearth Antiques
121 E. Thirty-fifth St.
New York, NY 10016
(212) 532-0535
By appointment or chance

Fine American antiques for the kitchen and dining room, including eighteenth- and nineteenth-century domestic accessories and painted country furniture.

Portico
379 W. Broadway
New York, NY 10012
(212) 941-7800

Home accessories and tableware in an eclectic mix of styles ranging from American Southwestern to French Country.

Pure Mädderlake
478 Broadway
New York, NY 10013
(212) 941-7770

Distinctive floral arrangements, plants, and wonderful containers mingle with home accessories and furnishings with a natural bent, such as beeswax candles and twig rockers.

D. F. Sanders & Co.
386 West Broadway
New York, NY 10012
(212) 925-9040

Everything from the table to the topping, including dishes, crystal, flatware, napery, and linens, all in an upbeat, eclectic style. Also at 952 Madison Ave.

The Store Next Door
943 Madison Ave.
New York, NY 10021
(212) 606-0200

Home accessories at the Whitney Museum's showcase shop include candlesticks, bowls, platters, and serving utensils that are creative both in design and in use of materials.

Terre Verde Trading Co.
72 Spring St.
New York, NY 10012
(212) 925-4533

Called an "ecological department store," this shop features objects such as glass jars made from recycled Coke bottles.

La Terrine
1024 Lexington Ave.
New York, NY 10021
(212) 988-3366

A wide range of hand-painted dinnerware and tableware from around the world, including complete place settings as well as accessory and decorative pieces. The Sweet Nellie Designs Cottage Rose pattern featured on p. 183 can be found at La Terrine. Also in Bridgehampton, NY.

Veen and Pol
399 Bleecker St.
New York, NY 10014
(212) 727-3988

An unusual selection of imported pots and containers as well as topiaries and occasional decorative accessories.

Wolfman Gold & Good Co.
116 Greene St.
New York, NY 10012
(212) 431-1888

For the mix-and-match table setter, white kitchen wares and tableware ranging from sturdy mugs to oversized platters as well as exclusive hand-painted dinnerware, unusual linens, and up-scale picnicware.

Zona
97 Greene St.
New York, NY 10012
(212) 925-6750

Earthy handcrafted home furnishings and table accessories, including plates, bowls, and candlesticks, as well as found objects.

NEW YORK STATE

Balasses House Antiques
Main St. and Hedges Lane
Amagansett, NY 11930
(516) 267-3032

Antique country furniture, especially English and French tables, and antique home and table accessories, including pottery, English cutlery, stemware, and serving pieces. The wooden tub, p. 104; carving set, p. 195; wine goblets, p. 195; butter dish, p. 195; keys, p. viii–1; and fish set, p. 12–13; all came from Balasses House Antiques.

Country Living
26 Montauk Highway
East Hampton, NY 11937
(516) 324-7371

Antique, reconstructed, and one-of-a-kind newly crafted cupboards and tables as well as folk art and home accessories.

Devonshire
Main St.
Bridgehampton, NY 11932
(516) 537-2661

New and antique garden furniture and home/garden accessories can be found in this English-style garden shop. Also in Middlebury, VT; Newport, RI; and Palm Beach, FL.

Wendy Engel Gallery
51 Main St.
East Hampton, NY 11937
(516) 324-6462

A wide selection of American crafts, baskets, unusual wood utensils, and pottery as well as African and Asian objects, including jewelry and textiles.

Fisher's Main St.
Main St.
Sag Harbor, NY 11963
(516) 725-0006

Furniture, including antique pine and fine reproduction tables, chairs, and cupboards. Some vintage tabletop and home accessories as well as new imported pottery, china, and dried floral arrangements. The egg stand featured on p. 183 came from this store.

Georgica Creek Antiques
Montauk Highway
Wainscott, NY 11975
(516) 537-0333

Country pieces, decorative china, textiles, and garden accessories such as the wheelbarrow seen on p. 94 can be found here.

The Grand Acquisitor
110 North Main St.
East Hampton, NY 11937
(516) 324-7272

An impressive collection of vintage and antique linens, including all sizes of tablecloths, runners, and napkins in damask, linen, and lace.

Kitchen Classics
Main St.
Bridgehampton, NY 11932
(516) 537-1111

Everything for the kitchen and well-dressed table, including handcrafted pottery, vintage objects, and unusual accessories. Items from Kitchen Classics featured in this book are the napkins, napkin rings, and antique wire stand on pp. 84–85; pitcher and glasses on p. 183; napkins and egg cups on p. 236; and paper-bag votives and torches on p. 245. Also in East Hampton.

C. W. Mercantile
Main St.
Bridgehampton, NY 11932
(516) 537-7914

For the table that is more country than formal, this shop offers French majolica, earthenware, and Portuguese ceramics; hand-painted dessert sets; French flatware; and linens.

Jay Moorhead Antiques
26 Montauk Highway
East Hampton, NY 11937
(516) 324-6819

For the more formal table, antique china, leaded crystal, and unusual pieces such as celery servers.

Polo Country Store
31–33 Main St.
East Hampton, NY 11937
(516) 324-1222

An ever-changing selection of folk art and vintage home and table accessories as well as new tableware from the Ralph Lauren Home Collection. The croquet set, p. 95, and the napkins, p. 148, came from this store.

Rank & Co.
4 Newtown Lane
East Hampton, NY 11937
(516) 324-7615

American primitive art and antiques, with furniture and occasional home and tabletop objects.

Gene Reed/Gene Reed Gallery
75 and 77 S. Broadway
Nyack, NY 10960
(914) 358-3750

Side by side, this shop and gallery offer international country tableware, decorative objects, and paintings in the shop, and high-end folk art, architectural items, and objects from the eighteenth century to the 1960s in the gallery. The Daniel Hale bird on p. 110 came from this gallery.

Saratoga Trunk Antiques
Montauk Highway
Amagansett, NY 11930
(516) 267-3583

American country objects, including vintage doors, windows, and beveled glass as well as decorative small objects such as baskets, glassware, and china. The picnic hamper featured on pp. 90–91 came from this shop.

Victory Garden
63 Main St.
East Hampton, NY 11937
(516) 324-7800

Table and home accessories with a French flavor, much bought in the French countryside, including Vallauris pottery, copper watering cans, huge olive-oil jars, and architectural elements.

White Pepper, Ltd.
23 Forest Ave.
Locust Valley, NY 11560
(516) 759-3650

Colorful and varied porcelain and ceramic dinnerware, including bowls and platters, as well as decorative objects for the home.

NORTH CAROLINA

Basketworks
Highway 107 South
Cashiers, NC 28717
(704) 743-5052

Unusual baskets for the home and table, many made of native materials, as well as twig and log tables.

Urban Artifacts
413 Forum VI
Greensboro, North Carolina 27408
(919) 855-0557

Architect- and artist-designed tabletop accessories by contemporary artisans, primarily American. Bridal registry available, as well as entertaining supplies for special events.

OKLAHOMA

T. A. Lorton
2046 Utica Square
Tulsa, OK 74114
(918) 743-1600

This tabletop and home-accessories shop offers hand-painted pottery, glass and stemware, French and hand-painted linens, unusual napkin rings, and antique small objects and furniture.

PENNSYLVANIA

Annex Cookery
5526 Walnut St.
Pittsburgh, PA 15232
(412) 621-6215

Offering everything from cookware and cooking lessons to the complete tabletop, this shop sells pot racks, baskets, hand-painted pottery, flatware, glassware, and even chocolates.

French Corner Antiques
130 Coulter Ave.
Ardmore, PA 19003
(215) 642-6867

Relaxed French Country eighteenth- and nineteenth-century dining furniture as well as decorative accessories such as ceramics and pottery, baskets, and copper vessels.

Sweet Violet
4361 Main St.
Philadelphia, PA 19127
(215) 483-2826

Displayed in English pine hutches, the tabletop and gift objects at this romantic shop include hand-painted pottery and hand-blown stemware.

Watermelon Blues
311 S. Craig St.
Pittsburgh, PA 15213
(412) 681-8451

New ceramic dinnerware, French doilies, linens, and other accessories for the table and home.

Wickens & Hicks, The American Store
43 Coulter Ave.
Ardmore, PA 19003
(215) 896-0504

American tabletop and home accessories, ranging from hand-painted dinnerware to blue zigzag ware, earthy mixing bowls, fruit-top canisters, and personalized wedding platters.

RHODE ISLAND

The Opulent Owl
295 S. Main St.
Providence, RI 02903
(401) 521-6698

Tableware, including hand-painted ceramic and china dinnerware and accessories, as well as decorative objects for the home.

Tropea-Puerini
39 Thames St.
Newport, RI 02840
(401) 846-3344

Limited-production home accessories and crafts, including colorful ceramic dinnerware and serving pieces.

Wickford Gourmet Kitchen & Table
31 W. Main St.
Wickford, RI 02864
(401) 295-9790

For the kitchen, stylish cookware, cutlery, and furniture; for the table, hand-painted dinnerware, decorative accessories, and table linens.

TEXAS

Jabberwocky
310 E. Main St.
Fredericksburg, TX 78624
(512) 997-7071

New and antique linens, ranging from lacy white tablecloths to sturdy cotton napery.

Surroundings
1708 Sunset Blvd.
Houston, TX 77005
(713) 527-9838

Formal country tableware and accessories for the patio, kitchen, and dining room, featuring mostly American handcrafted serving pieces and antique table and home accessories.

VERMONT

Simon Pearce
The Mill
Quechee, VT 05059
(802) 295-2711

Tableware, including hand-blown, hand-finished glass produced on site, as well as pottery, fine wooden bowls, and linens. Also in New York City.

Vermont Workshop
73 Central St.
Woodstock, VT 05091
(802) 457-1400

Wide-ranging tableware, including colorful plates and serving pieces, monogrammed glassware, painted furniture, and other home accessories.

VIRGINIA

Dovetails Antiques and Garden Accents
511 E. Water St.
Charlottesville, VA 22901
(804) 979-9955

Antique furnishings; weathered garden fixtures, including gates and mantels; and garden ornaments/accessories.

French Country Living
10205 Colvin Run Rd.
Great Falls, VA 22066
(703) 759-2245

Authentic French home accessories, including ceramics and tiles, fabrics, and furniture.

Gold Star Emporium
1027 Caroline St.
Fredericksburg, VA 22401
(703) 372-6448

Unique items for the home and garden, including exclusive hand work,

refinished antiques, kitchen items, lighting fixtures, and garden implements.

WASHINGTON

Sur La Table
84 Pine St.
Seattle, WA 98101
(206) 448-2244 and (800) 243-0852

This kitchen and tabletop shop carries French bistro flatware, Buffalo restaurant china, woodenware and copperware from France, English picnic baskets, and an extensive line of linens.

G. Swan
2025 First Ave.
Seattle, WA 98121
(206) 441-7950 and (800) 441-7950

In addition to offering collectible antique dishes, newly made hand-painted dinnerware, and linens, this shop offers workshops on home decor, including one on tablescapes.

In addition to the small, local shops that I love to visit, there are some national (and international) stores whose individual shops are so wonderful—and whose catalogs let us browse late at night—that they bear listing here.

Conran's Habitat	**Pierre Deux**
(800) 462-1769	*(800) 8-PIERRE*
Crate and Barrel	**Pottery Barn**
(800) 323-5461	*(800) 922-5507*
Fortune's Almanac	**Williams-Sonoma**
(800) 321-2232/2300	*(800) 541-2233*
Gump's	
(415) 982-1616	

List of Artisans

Some of the artisans mentioned in this book fill orders directly. Others are happy to suggest retail outlets where their work is sold. I regret that it was impossible to credit every handcrafted object and every talented artisan featured throughout these pages.

Joyce Ames
240 West 73rd St.
Suite 106
New York, NY 10023
(212) 799-8995

Annieglass Studio
303 Potero St. #8
Santa Cruz, CA 95060
(408) 426-5086

Roberta Bendavid
7 Park Ave.
New York, NY 10016
(212) 685-6247

Julie Cline
J.A. Cline Ceramics
3791 Harrison St.
Oakland, CA 94611
(415) 658-6515

Jimbo Davila
Rt. 5 Box 296AA
Santa Fe, NM 87501
(505) 455-2962

Barbara Eigen
Eigen Arts
150 Bay St.
Jersey City, NJ 07302
(201) 798-7310

Fioriware
26 N. 3rd St.
Zanesville, OH 43701
(614) 454-7400

Daniel M. Hale
718 Brookwood Rd.
Baltimore, MD 21229
(301) 233-5478

Ken Heitz
Box 161
Indian Lake, NY 12842
(518) 251-3327

Les Jones
General Delivery
Amagansett, NY 11930
(516) 267-8820

Eric Kirchner
Authentic Designs
West Rupert, VT 05776
(802) 394-7713

Judy Kogod
7325 Takoma Ave.
Takoma Park, MD 20912
(301) 588-3634

Robin Lankford
Folkheart
15005 Howe Rd.
Portland, MI 48875
(517) 647-6298

Andre LaPorte
Box 276
East Hampton, NY 11937
(516) 324-4288

Lindean Mill Glass
Galashiels
Selkirkshire TD1 3PE,
England
Telephone 0750 20173

Daniel Mack
3280 Broadway, 3rd fl.
New York, NY 10027
(212) 926-3880

MacKenzie-Childs Ltd.
Aurora, NY 13026
(315) 364-7131

Gary S. Magakis
1129 N. Third St.
Philadelphia, PA 19123
(215) 625-0157

Donna McGee
East Street Clay Studios
47 East St.
Hadley, MA 01035
(413) 584-0508

Charles H. Muise, Jr.
47 West 8th St.
New York, NY 10011
(212) 473-5502

Ann Marie Murray & Co.
1804 Wrightfield Ave.
Yardley, PA 19067
(215) 493-4614

Simon Pearce Glass
The Mill
Quechee, VT 05059
(802) 295-2711

Carol Pflumm
The Herb Farm
Barnard Road
Granville, MA 01034
(413) 357-8882

Melinda Reed
Fox Hill Furniture Co.
11 Smith Neck Rd.
Old Lyme, CT 06371
(203) 434-3071

Claudia Reese
2816 Saratoga
Austin, TX 78733
(512) 263-5018

Susan Ryan
Seaberry-Taylor-Ryan
680 Randall Rd.
Santa Barbara, CA 93108
(805) 969-6460

Arabelle Taggart
350 E. 91st St.
New York, NY 10128
(212) 860-2833

Two Women Boxing
3002-B Commerce St.
Dallas, TX 75226
(214) 939-1626

Liz Wain
230 Fifth Ave.
New York, NY 10010
(212) 679-9540

Recipe Index

Breakfast and Brunch

Bountiful Board French Toast	265
Egg-and-Sausage Soufflé	245
Smoked Salmon and Leek Frittata	259

Breads

Buttermilk Corn Sticks	259
Easy Rosemary Focaccia	256
Lazy Banana Blueberry Muffins	248

Appetizers

Fancy Baked Brie	252
Lemon Shrimp	258
Mock Foie Gras	251
Roquefort-Yogurt Puree en Endive	258
Spicy Tuna Tartare	258
Zesty Melon Salsa	264

Soups

Chicken and Shrimp Gumbo	250
Cold Beet Soup	253
Exotic Gazpacho	266
Pumpkin Peanut Soup	264

Vegetables

Ginger Beets	261
New Potatoes with Rosemary	263
Sesame Green Beans	262
Stuffed Potato Choices	264
Sweet Potatoes with Marshmallows	252
Winter Vegetable Casserole	249

Salads and Dressings

Celestial Salad with Pommery Vinaigrette	250
Cherry Tomato and Blue Cheese Salad	266
Confetti Coleslaw	251
Curried Egg Salad	253
Cucumbers with Yogurt-Dill Dressing	261
Marinated Cherry Tomatoes	260
Minnie K.'s Jell-O–Carrot Salad	252
Northern White Bean Salad	255
Papaya Salad with Tangy Dressing	248
Southwestern Salad with Tangy Vinaigrette	263
Special Salad Dressing	254
Tempting Tuna Salad	253
Wild Rice Salad with Avocado and Tahini Dressing	261

Lunch and Dinner Entrees

American Crab Cakes	249
Asparagus-Stuffed Chicken Breasts with Prosciutto and Goat Cheese	257
Barefoot Contessa Turkey Breast with Spinach Stuffing	260
Chicken Salad with Grapes	254
E.G.H. Pasta	256
Grilled Mixed Sausages with Sweet Peppers	262
Grilled Swordfish Steaks with Red Pepper Sauce	261
Grilled Vegetable-and-Cheese Sandwiches	252

Desserts

Center-Stage Chocolate Cake	263
Chocolate Nut Cookies	265
Ina's Bread Pudding	260
Lemon Glaze	251
Moist Applesauce Chunkies	255
Mom's Sugar Cookies	262
Old-Fashioned Lemon-Almond Sugar Cookies	257
Peach Walnut Crisp	251
Spirited Chocolate-Chip Cookies	255
Sweet Finale Toffee Bars	253

Beverages

Orange Spice Tea	259
Swedish Glögg	264

Miscellaneous/Special

Amanda's Doggie Treats	254
Beach Clambake	266
Flavored Herb Butter	257
Garlic-Herb Vinegar	265
Preserved Eggplant	265